WINE SOMMELIER

A JOURNEY THROUGH THE CULTURE OF WINE

GREAT IS THE FORTUNE
OF HE WHO POSSESSES
A GOOD BOTTLE,
A GOOD BOOK,
A GOOD FRIEND.

Molière

WHITE STAR PUBLISHERS

Project editor LAURA ACCOMAZZO

Graphic design MARIA CUCCHI

PHOTOGRAPHS BY FABIO PETRONI

TEXT BY JACOPO COSSATER

CONTENTS

PREFACE

No other man-produced drink in the world has populated – and continues to populate – the writing world as much as wine, with an unrestrained bibliography that dates back to the birth of writing itself. It couldn't be any different: wine has been the perfect pairing to meals and important celebrations in the western world for thousands of years; in many countries it is not just a drink, it is a unique cultural element.

The beauty of wine has therefore to be traced in its history and its diffusion from Persia to the Mediterranean basin, progressively expanding into the rest of the world. During such an exciting journey, a huge number of wine varietals were born – although today the most famous ones are barely more than a few dozen – as well as innumerable different wines. This is it: wine is always going to be unique. No bottle of wine can ever be identical to another, no matter how far or close from each other they are produced, nor can it be replicated in exactly the same way. Each harvest has its own history and delivers ever-changing elements to the table – elements that are the result of a constant dialog between the vineyard, the territory where it is cultivated and human work, through actions and choices rooted in the traditions of that particular area. It's the *terroir*, the timbre of each wine, which represents the region of production along with its overall characteristics, always unequalled anywhere else.

This book was conceived to admire this uniqueness and is directed at those who want an introduction to the world of wine step by step. By using understandable language, it aims to reveal some of the most iconic wines in the world. Whether they are white, red, sparkling, sweet, or fortified, these wines have an extremely tight bond with their territory, about which they can tell the fascinating history. Such an indissoluble relationship explains why it has become common to look especially at Europe as the birthplace of contemporary wine – particularly in France, Italy and Spain, as countries that above any other can bring a vast number of prestigious wines, with each region basically producing its own. However, countries like Germany, Austria, Portugal and Hungary pride themselves on their unforgettable wines too, not to mention the United States, Canada, South Africa and Chile; despite being very distant from one another, they have only made their entrance into the wine market in the last few centuries and are progressively uncovering their uniqueness.

Wines can be produced in millions of bottles or in just a few thousands, but they always retain the richness of their personality.

Let's go and discover them together.

WINE THROUGH HISTORY; A THOUSANDS OF YEARS-OLD STORY

WINE IN THE ANCIENT WORLD

The history of wine dates back to the beginning of time and coincides with the birth and development of the most important human civilizations. According to some studies, the *Vitis vinifera*, i.e. the vine plant whose fruits are suitable for vinification, would already spontaneously grow in the area between the modern Iran and the southeastern Mediterranean ten thousand years ago. It is impossible to date precisely the moment in which someone realized how pleasant that alcoholic drink resulting from must fermentation was; however it is certain that a goblet containing what could have been wine appeared in Sumerian, Babylonian and even Egyptian art.

The amount of evidence that can be found today increases significantly with Ancient Greece and, more consistently, with the Romans. Rome was the capital that has contributed more than any other to the development of wine. Wine has always been linked to spirituality and worshiping gods: for the Jews, Noah was the first ever wine maker and his Ark certainly contained some vine branches. The Greeks and Romans worshiped Dionysus and Bacchus, as representations of the ecstasy of life as well as symbols of human existence itself. Then came the Christians who gave wine a central role within the Eucharist.

Thanks to the numerous survived texts, we know that the Roman upper classes could afford long-lived wines, aged even for decades. They were mainly sweet with the addition of aromatic ingredients, probably rather alcoholic and therefore quite long-lived; they were stored in medium-sized terracotta amphorae. The rest of the population had access to a simpler wine from the most recent harvest, less alcoholic and probably more similar to the wine we know today. Everybody would drink, which is what led the Romans to create proper production protocols and to give an extraordinary input to viticulture and to the foundation of what would become the modern vineyard.

More importantly the Romans brought the vine plants to any territory they conquered: Spain, in the south and then in the north of France, followed by Germany and England. There was no region of the Empire that didn't produce its own wine, compatibly with the climatic conditions. In order to transport it, the vineyards would be planted next to rivers, as they were the natural transport links that the Romans were experts in using. That is how some of the legendary wine making areas were born – Bordeaux, Champagne, the Lore Valley, Mosel and Rioja.

WINE TODAY

It is hard to identify a moment in history when wine acquired those characteristics we know it for today. It was a long process, starting in the 1600s and lasting for almost 2 centuries. However, at least one factor contributed significantly to changing its taste and its consumption: the invention of the glass bottle in England. Up to that moment, wine had been stored inside a variety of different containers; since Roman times, it had been stored in wooden barrels or terracotta amphorae, to be poured into a decanter or inside a small leather bag for serving. At the beginning of the 17th century, the progress of the glass industry allowed to make bottles that were less fragile and much cheaper. They were quite different to the ones we know today – their base was ball-shaped – but still perfect for the function they were designed for, i.e. storing and transporting. England had huge interests in the wine business; many English tradesmen had settled in harbor centers such as Porto (Portugal), Marsala (Italy) and Jerez de la Frontera (Spain), contributing to make those wines famous at home. Another important center was Bordeaux, a region with which strong commercial contacts had been built over the years, not to mention those areas overseas where rum was produced. England maintained its central role for a very long time, becoming the most important wine market in the world, despite not being a country of production.

With the introduction of glass bottles the first aged wines started to become popular, for they were more structured than the red wines so popular in previous centuries. It was soon understood that a well-sealed wine could maintain itself better and also develop more pleasant aromas with the passing of time. It was at the beginning of the 1700s that the contemporary geography of wine was born. Bordeaux established its leadership thanks also to the extensive commercial routes previously built. Furthermore a new region emerged, quickly gaining importance: Burgundy. The 18th century saw wine becoming the absolute protagonist all over Europe both from a commercial and production point of view; every region had its own specialty and that is when we saw the first examples of some of the most appreciated and popular denominations, in Italy, Spain, Germany and other major wine making countries.

However everything changed in the second half of the 1800s. The more and more popular practice of importing American vines to plant in Europe sparked the biggest vine disease that history has ever known. A tiny insect called Phylloxera literally wiped out most part of the vineyards of the Old Continent, as they were not resistant to the parasite. It was an utter disaster, entire economies collapsed and it took several decades to find and circulate a solution that permitted the cultivations take off again.

The following era saw what could be called a rebirth of wine; during the 20th century the wine making world saw 2 important conquests. The first had to do with the crucial discoveries of the French chemist Louis Pasteur, allowing a better understanding of the function of yeasts during the alcoholic fermentation. The second related to the growing popularity of refrigeration systems that led to the establishment of new production areas, especially in the New World. It is no coincidence that starting from the end of the Second World War new areas blossomed, such as California, Australia and South America, with their wineries able to impose themselves on the market both thanks to wines that respected the French tradition and the diffusion of easily replicable production standards. After seeing what were often "caricature" wines appearing on the market during the 1980s and 1990s – made more to show off than to be truly enjoyed – today it looks like we are back to those traditions that built the prestige of the wine making areas in the world, and it is a common opinion that we haven't enjoyed the company of outstanding wines as much as we are doing now.

WINE IN THE WORLD

The ideal conditions for the cultivation of the vine plant are between the 30th and the 50th parallel, both in the northern and southern hemisphere, where all the most important wine making areas worldwide are located. In the northern hemisphere, these parallels include most of Europe, from the French Champagne to Sicily in Italy, as well as the United States, Canada and China – this has been significantly growing in recent years, especially from a numerical point of view. Such a map has many exceptions, due to the climate of certain regions as well as to the global warming process, which for instance is permitting the production of some interesting white and sparkling wines in England, where all wine for consumption had been imported up to recent years.

Europe still is the heart of wine production worldwide. Its leadership relates to numbers – Italy, France, Spain, Portugal and Germany produce more wine than the rest of the world put together – as well as to quality, if looking at the average value per bottle. However in the latest decades the countries of the so-called New World have made giant steps by not only producing single bottles of exceptional wine but also by creating an extremely lively and promising productive fabric.

Apart from the West Coast – where the history of a good number of production entities dates back to the 19th century – there are many US states with a well-established wine making industry; Michigan, Oregon, Washington and New York are amongst the most important. In South America, apart from the already mentioned Chile and Argentina, countries like Brazil with its enormous potential or Uruguay are making themselves noticed. South Africa has been at the center of the stage for many decades and it has no intention to stop, thanks to a new generation of attentive wine makers who are showing how unexplored the country still is from a production point of view. Last but not least, Australia and New Zealand have started to systematically cultivate the vine thanks to the settlers who began to do so at the end of the 19th century and are now becoming possibly the most interesting in the New World. Victoria, New south Wales, South Australia and Queensland are fascinating regions for their naturalistic beauty and above all for their suitability to wine production. The thousands of bottles that are opened all over the world every year prove it.

16

THE VINEYARD FIRST, THEN THE CELLAR; IT IS THE BIRTH OF WINE

THE VINEYARD

Each wine is the extraordinary result of three essential elements. The first is the individuality of the place where it is born and produced; sometimes it is enough to walk just a few hundred meters further to come across a completely different context – especially the terrain and microclimate, which are crucial dynamics to the production of any wine. The second has to do with the varietal: although often cultivated one next to the other, Pinto Nero, Sangiovese, Cabernet Sauvignon, Nebbiolo, Chardonnay, Trebbiano and so on can produce very different wines. The third and last is the human component: man's work and choices first in the vineyards and then in the winery have a profound effect on the final outcome, through a process that often refers back to cultural centuries-long traditions. It is a truly virtuous triangle where each component is inseparable from the others.

What is mostly surprising is that such an incredible variety comes from the fruit of a single plant, the vine. This is the magic of wine: no other fruit plant – for example, the apple tree and cider, the result of the fermentation of apple juice – is able to give such a good and versatile drink: white, rose, red, more or less colorful, more or less fragranced, more or less bodied and long-lived, always capable of being unforgettable.

The diversity always begins in the vineyard, i.e. the place where the vine plant completes its vegetative cycle and the grapes reach a full ripening. It is a very important place, whose characteristics are central for the quality of the future wine. The most beautiful vineyards are generally located uphill rather than on flat terrain, where the excessive humidity develops into mists. At the same time a good vineyard needs good sun exposure, so that the leaves can benefit from the light necessary for photosynthesis. The vines need vast water resources to guarantee the quality of the grapes – that is why areas that are too drought-prone are not suitable – but they need to be shielded from the elements at the same time. In fact, one single hailstorm or a rainless season can compromise and destroy a whole harvest.

Any wine is linked to sun and rain; the grapes are mainly made of water that the plant absorbs from the terrain, as well of the sugar resulting from photosynthesis. The process has a beginning and an end: during the first years of life, the vine spends all its energies to grow and become stronger. Only from the third or fourth year on is it possible to use its grapes. With age and the progressive growth of the roots apparatus, the grapes become better and better, delivering wines that are increasingly complex and deep. Finally, after 25/30 years, the plant decreases its yields.

However grapes coming from a very old vineyard are considered prestigious and ideal for the production of a great wine. That is why it is always difficult to establish when is the best moment to uproot it and start all over again; it is a calculation that in some cases goes beyond a pure economical evaluation.

Everything stems from the vineyard and any decision has a direct consequence; first on the grapes and then on the wine. This has also to do with the uniqueness of the wine, as a product that is never perfectly repeatable, for it is always the result of different harvests – different because of the climatic trend and human choices about the type of machinery, pruning and harvesting.

HARVEST AND VINIFICATION

The vegetative cycle of the vine starts in March in the northern hemisphere and in September in the southern. During this period and after the winter pruning, the first buds peek out as shy green hints of what will later be the grapes. Immediately after, the leaves grow and after a few weeks the flowers emerge; tiny bunches of little flowers that will turn into grapes. It is a delicate phase that even one single frost can compromise. With the passing weeks, the grapes acquire their familiar shape and begin changing color – from green to red for instance – reaching a full ripening. It is time to pick them.

The right time to harvest and to take the grapes to the winery is always variable. It is a very difficult decision that changes from one area to another and even from one winery to another. Before harvesting, the wine maker keeps an eye on certain factors, such as the level of sugar and acid in the grapes. These factors are highly influenced by the weather; it is always better to harvest on a nice day than when there could be a storm. Too prolonged rains can endanger the quality of the harvest. Even an excessively hot day can affect the following vinification; in some areas it is preferred to harvest at night so as to take the grapes to the winery at the optimal temperature to be vinificated.

Any winery lives the harvest season as the most frenetic of the whole year; a constant coming and going of tractors transporting containers full of freshly picked grapes ready to be processed. Without counting the best modern technologies, the main steps of the vinification haven't changed. The grapes are poured into a big destemming machine that separates the grapes from the stems and leaves. The mix of skins and pulp that comes out is ready to be pressed – the same pressing process, done with the feet for centuries, which has been represented in all civilizations that have engaged in wine production. The must is then placed in big containers where it starts one of its most delicate phases: fermentation. Wine is by definition the product of fermentation, i.e. when the yeasts inside the must turn the sugar into alcohol and carbon dioxide that will then disperse in the air. That is why, generally speaking, countries with a hotter climate produce more alcoholic wines, because of the presence of sugar in the grapes. This phase can last a few days or many weeks depending on different

factors, all linked to the crucial role of temperatures. Once this process is terminated, the wine is still far from being ready; before being bottled, it needs to rest and age for a certain period of time.

AGING

Once the must has turned into wine, especially in the case of red wines, a secondary fermentation is necessary, called malolactic fermentation; it involves the action of specific bacteria that transform the malic acid, with its pungent and strong taste, into the softer lactic acid. Then the wine starts changing its organoleptic characteristics: the color usually becomes paler, the fragrances become richer and purer and the taste gains roundness and balance. Regardless of its duration, aging almost always takes place in oak barrels, especially for more ambitious wines. Oak is a particularly popular type of wood – unlike chestnut, cherry and acacia – because of its limited invasiveness, which is ideal to let the wine "breathe", i.e. to have constant contact with oxygen without the wine's aromas being too influenced by the natural odors of the wood.

The most prestigious barrels come from France, a country that boasts a centuries-long tradition in the sector; however new barrels coming from the United States and more in general from countries capable to compete with their cheaper prices, have recently made their entrance into the market. The barrels coming from Slavonia are just as important, as their big dimensions are suitable for long aging periods. Barrels come in the most diverse sizes: the Barrique is widely popular, with a capacity of 225 liters, as well as the Tonneau, with a capacity of 300-500 liters. Quality is just as important – if not more so – as capacity; the best barrels require a production process that can last several years. The wooden staves are left in the open air to disperse all those strong aromas. It is obviously possible to leave the wine to rest in other containers; just think that Georgia – one of the areas with the longest wine making tradition – still uses big and fascinating clay amphorae, a type of container that is having a growing success all over the world.

The wine not only improves its organoleptic qualities whilst aging, but it also becomes more and more stable until it's time for it to be bottled (this time depends either on the rules dictated by the specific product specification or on the wine maker's decision). The wine is now ready for the last leg of its journey in the glass bottle; a more or less long rest in the winery in order to settle once for all, before being commercialized and tasted from our glasses.

THE GLASS FROM EVERY ANGLE; SUGGESTIONS AND PAIRING

Tasting any wine is an extraordinary discovery that involves a fascinating number of factors, such as history, geography and the human touch. It is an in-depth study that should be experienced with curiosity and an open mind. Each wine has the ability to amaze even the most experienced taster and it constantly reminds us of what a special drink it is – unique and unrepeatable, as it immortalizes a moment and a place that might change its deepest traits after just a few weeks. Conventionally the tasting of any drink, including wine, can be divided into three moments: visual, olfactory and taste. They remain separated only for an instant, to then blend, resulting in the mosaic of sensations that each wine represents, whether white or red.

VISUAL ANALYSIS

This is the first contact with a wine, during which the taster can start forming an idea of what they will discover with their nose and then in their mouth. The appearance of any wine can reveal precious information not only about its evolution process but also about its structure and its type. In extreme cases, if the color for example appears to be too dull, the tasting might not go further, as the wine has almost certainly completed its evolutionary curve. The grape skin is responsible for the color of the wine, which during vinification remains in contact with the must for a variable period of time. That is why rose wines, which remain in contact with the skins for just a short period, have such a characteristic color. The same can be said for certain white wines that are left in contact with their skins for a long time: their color will tend towards an amber hue, darker than "normal" whites. Different varietals produce different colors; Pinot Nero and Nebbiolo contain less colorants than Merlot and Cabernet Sauvignon. That is why the visual examination can give useful information about the wine in the glass.

After pouring it into the glass – never more than a third of the volume of the glass – attention moves to the color, which can be best examined if put against a light background for a few seconds (a white napkin is perfect). Younger wines always have very brilliant colors; in the case of red wines, the color fades over time, whereas whites tend to become darker. The important thing is to check how the color can vary in its transparency from the center of the glass up to its sides. It is there that the action of time will reveal more clearly its chromatic variations; red wines in particular tend towards garnet and orange shades.

However the most important factor is the quality of the color itself, i.e. the way the wine refracts the light. A bright vivid wine will most probably be pleasantly intense, good and balanced.

The visual examination doesn't stop with the color; for instance, if a wine moves rapidly inside the glass, leaving thick streaks down the inside of the glass, it will most probably be a rather alcoholic wine. Even its consistency – more or less fluid – helps to contextualize its structure. And then are the bubbles: in the case of sparkling wines it is simply beautiful to contemplate that apparently magical phenomenon of a natural effervescence. In this case there are many elements to keep an eye on; for instance the foam created once poured into the glass has to be fine and dry, and should disappear almost immediately. The bubbles are better if abundant, with the exception of particularly aged sparkling wines. The smaller they are, the better, as well as their persistence – they should remain dense even after a few minutes inside the glass. As with any other wine, there is one universal rule: the better it looks, the better it is. A great sparkling wine has in fact a very fine and abundant perlage (bubbles) which doesn't "explode" in the glass but instead leave the bubbles to rise up to the surface in their own time, with grace and elegance.

Generally used on festive occasions, the flute is the most famous glass for sparkling wines.

Thanks to its tulip shape, it helps to detect the different nuances of the best sparkling wines with more precision.

As a greatly versatile glass, it is suitable for particularly complex red wines.

Widely used for Pinot Noir, it is a glass suitable for very refined red wines, with great olfactory complexity.

Its specific shape makes it suitable for a long-aged wine and perfect for experiencing all its nuances.

Perfect for everyday use, it is suitable for white wines as well as for the simplest reds.

Thin and slim, it is a glass suitable for the freshest white wines.

A widely popular glass, it is used to serve the majority of white wines.

Thanks to its shape, it is a glass suitable for tasting more structured white wines.

Very versatile glass, it is suitable for tasting fortified wines.

A widely popular glass, it is suitable for sweeter wines.

Created specifically for Sauternes wines, today it is used for more complex sweet wines.

OLFACTORY EXAMINATION

This is the phase during which the nose tries to capture the fragrances in the wine, not only in their intensity and quantity but also and most importantly in their quality. The first smell should always be followed by a second longer one, preferably after gently swirling the wine inside the glass. Such a delicate movement increases the surface of the wine that has contact with air, therefore releasing a higher number of aromatic compounds. The more intense the perceived sensations are, the stronger the wine's aroma. It is a process that in the most complex cases requires time and concentration; it is not rare to come across wines that can deliver olfactory sensations that are very diverse after a few minutes, especially if left to age in the cellar for a long time.

The olfactory examination is the phase that requires the most experience and training within the tasting process. Years and years of practice are needed to build a proper olfactory archive of aromas and scents that can help to interpret the innermost qualities of a wine, from its origins to its evolutionary status. It is the most challenging step of the tasting adventure for a novice, especially at the beginning. A wine should not be experienced and evaluated as a single entity, but as an ensemble of distinct elements that together create its fragrance. It is useful to try and memorize just a few fragrances to learn to recognize them in different wines. Cherry, blackberry, lemon and peach are a few of the fruit-based aromas that are frequently detectable. Some professional tasters also train themselves through "sniffing around", thereby educating their olfactory sense to recognize different scents within different contexts.

Conventionally the aromas of a wine are divided into 3 categories: primary, secondary and tertiary. The primary come directly from the grape varietal; aromas that can be easily traced back by picking a single grape, opening it and smelling it. Obviously not all wine varietals smell the same and those that have the most intense aromas are called aromatic; once vinificated, Gewürztraminer, Müller-Thurgau and in a minor way, Riesling and Chardonnay deliver bouquets that can be easily found in the glass. The secondary aromas are closely linked to the chemical process of the transformation of the must into wine, therefore produced during fermentation. They include notes that can even be very distant from one another and include different categories of fragrances: fruit, fruit jam, white flowers, red, yellow flowers and honey that are closely linked to the practices followed during production, above all the fermentation temperature. However the aromas that can be found in the glass go beyond these; during the aging process, the fragrances inside the wine continue to change. Not only do they develop, new scents that are closely related to this phase also come to life. They are also often influenced by the container in which the wine is left to rest, i.e. oak barrels that can give off toasted vanilla scents.

That which makes this world of aromas so fascinating, is that each fragrance, or almost, has a more-or-less direct link with the varietal from which the wine is born; with the place and way in which it is produced. Notes of green pepper will therefore lead us to red wines originating from Cabernet Sauvignon, hints of violet to Nebbiolo, of butter to Chardonnay; to mention just a few of the most famous. A world of fragrances to discover.

GUSTATORY ANALYSIS

This is the most important part of tasting, where previous suppositions are either confirmed or proved wrong. If the sense of smell can perceive the aromas of the wine, the mouth can clearly distinguish all its essential components: the softer and harder parts, the sweetness and sapidity, the bitterness, acidity and persistence. A small sip of wine comes in contact with the tongue and the palate, where it stays for a few seconds to reach all the receptors in the mouth, to be finally swallowed. During this moment it is possible to assess all the elements needed to understand the gustatory behavior of the wine, its overall balance and its true "substance".

The categories of flavors that the mouth can identify are 4: sweet, savory, acid and bitter. The sweetness is linked to the sugar contained in the wine; it is easily recognizable, especially in dessert wines. When the sugar residue inside a wine is below a certain threshold, then the palate perceives a certain roundness. Roundness is a quality that is present in all wines – sparkling, white and red – and it can be more or less accentuated depending on the type of wine. It makes the wine velvety. Sapidity, as the word says, relates to the salts in the wine and the palate senses slight minerality, a peculiarity of certain wines. Acidity, typical of citrus for instance, relates to the acids inside the wine and it determines a stronger or lighter freshness; it is an essential quality that counterbalances the roundness. Bitterness recalls a bitter sensation that is quite rare in wines and that shouldn't be confused with astringency. Apart from the 4 main flavors, the palate can detect a range of so-called tactile sensations that have to do with the texture of the wine. The tannins, especially in red wines, provoke a certain contraction of the gums along with a sensation of dryness, i.e. astringency. Other tactile sensations are warmth, linked to the alcoholic content of the wine, and roundness, to which poly-alcohols like glycerin contribute. All these characteristics can be confusing at the beginning, but with a bit of training they become very easy to detect and altogether they determine the body of the wine. They have to be assessed singularly but evaluated as part of an ensemble: from their perfect balance comes the best wines.

Finally, the persistence of the wine is essential, i.e. the array of sensations that remain on the palate after drinking and that can fade very slowly in the best cases. Persistence doesn't have to do only with how long the wine takes to disappear in the mouth, but also and most importantly with the quality of its aromas. A particularly astringent wine that is rich with tannins and leaves an excessively bitter and possibly long trace, is in most cases a poorly balanced red; too unbalanced towards its hardest traits. That is why persistence can't be judged only in chronological terms but as an overall of different features; intensity, overall pleasantness and elegance. A common trait of all great wines is the ability of leaving behind an immensely pleasant memory that inevitably invites the taster to come back to their glass for a further sip.

PAIRING

If tasting is a fascinating journey to the discovery of wine, the journey that analyzes its relationship with food is just as stimulating. Each dish enjoys a pairing with a specific wine that can enhance certain characteristics. It is no coincidence: wine is extraordinary exactly because it is so versatile and can include an impressive range of aromas and flavors that can intertwine in endless combinations, like no other drink in the world can do. It is a true minister, or servant: the best wines can manage each nuance of a dish, empowering its gustatory profile in a guaranteed charming bond.

It is quite clear at what moment in history wine made its appearance on the table – it is certain for instance that in the ancient Greek culture it was a custom to drink wine after dinner, diluting it with warm water – however it is more uncertain when it started to accompany everyday meals. It was possibly a gradual process: the Romans for example were known to drink simpler wines before a meal and to enjoy more bodied wines afterwards – often sweet and with the addition of honey and spices; an order of consuming wine that has remained unchanged ever since. The first written proof about pairings is by the famous historian and geographer Sante Lancerio, who was the sommelier of Pope Paul III: in around the mid-16th century he was responsible for the wine supplies for His Holiness and he kept a diary where he would make a note of the unique peculiarities of each wine he would come across, often along with gastronomical suggestions, i.e. pairings. At that time each region and city could almost exclusively count on the wines produced in the surrounding territories and they were naturally paired with the typical local dishes. That is how some valid pairings were born, related to tradition and seasons. They are the result of centuries of family customs, adapting to each other over time. It is well worth studying this aspect more in depth during any trip or visit to a new region; the most typical local dish will most probably pair with the local wine for everyday consumption.

Pairing food with wine requires experience and training; an additional or missing ingredient can change not only the taste of a dish but also its characteristics. At the same time, although there are quite precise rules on the subject, it is always good to let oneself be guided by instinct and gustatory memory; it is common to come across pairings that could appear as a bit stretched on paper, but that reveal to be winners in reality.

A successful pairing doesn't just promote a dish, it also makes the desire for the food and wine stay vivid and alive; basically that which, after a first sip and a first mouthful, invites you to taste again, and again. There are many exceptions and tricky dishes, if not impossible, to pair in a satisfactory way – dishes rich in lemon or vinegar are a valid example. However a few simple general rules can help to create a good pairing, by playing with the concepts of concordance and juxtaposition, the marriage and contrast between some of the characteristics of the wine and the food. An example of concordance is evident with desserts, which have always to be paired with sweet wines, contrary to the custom of often ending a meal with a cake and a dry sparkling wine. The same can be said for the structure of the food, i.e. elements that have to "walk" alongside each other, without one being penalized over the other; a dish that is too rich can overpower a weaker wine, and vice versa.

In order to pair a wine correctly it is necessary to know the characteristics of the dishes as well as those of the wines, in order for them to create great pleasure together.

Here are some useful guidelines:

✍ The tendency of a dish to be particularly fatty, with a tactile sensation of a certain mellowness in the mouth and a certain patina-like feeling on the tongue, can positively balance with wines that boast a marked sapidity or effervescence, i.e. sparkling wines. This is the case for cheese, cold meats and some types of meat.

✍ The tendency of a dish to be mildly sweet and reasonably soft easily balances with strongly acidic wines, even though sapidity and effervescence can play a significant role. This is the case for risotto, pasta, potatoes and legume-based dishes, as well as crustaceans.

✍ The tendency of a dish to be succulent, with a tactile sensation of the presence of liquids in the mouth, easily balances with rather alcoholic wines, with a good tannic texture. This is the case for rare-chargrilled, braised and stewed meat.

✍ The tendency of a dish to be particularly greasy, with a tactile sensation of being slippery in the mouth, easily balances with rather alcoholic wines. This is the case for dishes rich with butter, oil, pork and baked sausages.

✍ The tendency of a dish to be particularly acid and, above all, savory is well balanced by wines with a certain alcoholic content. This is the case for tomato-based dishes, grilled fish and marinated meat.

✍ The tendency of a dish to be bitter can be well-balanced by soft and moderately alcoholic wines. This is the case for certain types of cheese, certain vegetables, grilled fish and offal.

In any case it is entertaining to try new unpredicted pairings, by just following experience and one's gustatory memory; it is a rare discovery through one's senses.

FROM THE SILENCE OF THE CELLAR TO THE ENTERTAINMENT AT THE TABLE

THE BOTTLE

There are many different shapes of bottles on the market: tall, short and more or less capacious. Their shape is functional to a specific purpose. That used for sparkling wine for instance, commonly known as a "Champagne bottle", boasts a thicker glass designed to absorb the pressure coming from the build-up of carbon dioxide inside. The so-called "Burgonet" – popular especially in the French region of Burgundy – has a fairly pronounced "shoulder" that prevents the sediments from being poured out during serving. The same can be said for the Bordeaux, which is absolutely the most popular, and for the Albeisa, typical of the region of Langhe in Piedmont (Italy). Almost all wine making regions have developed a common bottle over the years, for instance the famous Alsatian and the one from the Rhine Valley, used for white wines in both regions. Wine is the drink whose essence lies in conviviality, as it is evident for those so-called big sizes: a double bottle is called Magnum (1.5 liters). Even bigger are the Jéoroboam (3 liters) and the Mathusalem (6 liters), up to those sizes suitable for particular events: bottles of over 15 liters capacity!

Opening a bottle of wine shouldn't pose any difficulty if using a good cork-screw. There are many types and models on the market, but the most popular and reliable is the sommelier knife. Light, handy and entirely made of steel, it features a double step on the lever to facilitate the extraction of the cork.

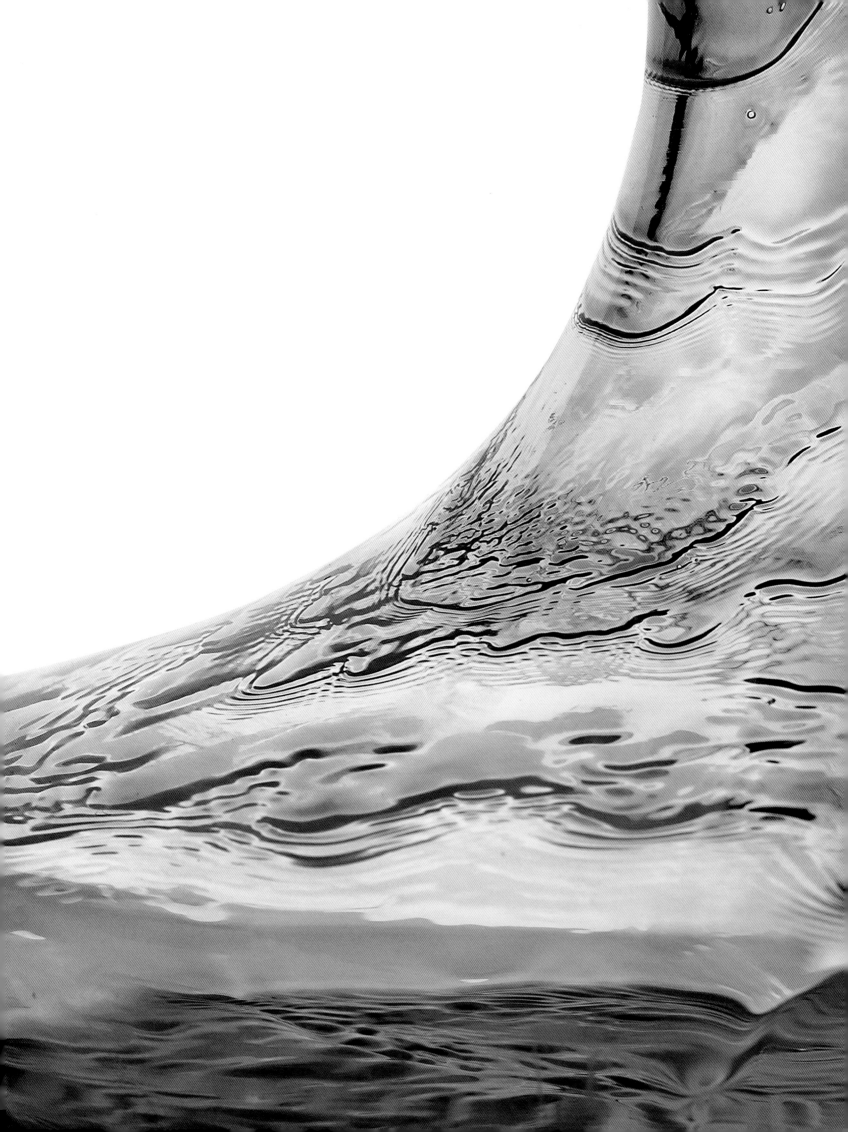

Today cork is still the most common material for quality wines in Europe. However alternative types of capping are emerging on the market, such as the screw cap. There is an ongoing discussion about this but what is certain is that more simple wines, i.e. those consumed within a few months or years, the screw cap is a perfectly suitable solution. Better still, it eliminates any possible contamination due to defective corks and is therefore seeing a growing appreciation amongst wine producers.

Particular attention must be paid in the case of particularly aged bottles, as the wine, especially reds, might form a certain amount of sediment. In these cases, a decanter can be useful to help a speedy oxygenation of the drink. In case of very "fragile" wines – that could suffer from sudden contact with air – it is best to keep the bottle upright for a few hours before serving to help the sediment sit at the bottom, and then open the bottle with extreme care.

BORDEAUX BOTTLE: from the name sake French region, it has progressively become the world's most popular wine bottle

BORDEAUX BOTTLE, HIGH SHOULDER: used for certain prestigious red and white wines

BORDEAUX BOTTLE, HIGH SHOULDER: in its smaller version of 0.375 liters capacity, it is the most popular for a wide variety of sweet wines

BURGUNDY BOTTLE: from the name sake French region, it is used for both white and red wines

ALBEISA: from the region of Langhe in Piedmont (Italy), it is particularly used for Barolo and Barbaresco wines

RHINE BOTTLE: typical of Germany, it has become synonymous with Riesling wine

CHAMPAGNE BOTTLE: used all over the world for a variety of sparkling wines, not just for Champagne

CHAMPAGNE BOTTLE PRESTIGE CUVÉE: with its more pronounced shapes, it is used for the highest class of Champagne wines

MARSALA BOTTLE: from the name sake Sicilian town in Italy, its centuries-old shape has remained unchanged throughout time

PORTO BOTTLE: from the name sake Portuguese town, its particularly pronounced shoulder avoids sediments to be poured into the glass when serving

PROVENÇAL BOTTLE: although increasingly rare, it is used for the delicate rosé wines produced in the south of France

CLAVELIN: used only in the French region of Jura, it is synonymous with *Vin Jaune* (young wine)

SERVING TEMPERATURES

The temperature range to best appreciate the characteristics of a wine is quite wide, starting at 6/8°C for the simplest sparkling wines and arriving at 18/20°C for the most aged reds. Tasting a white wine which is too warm can enhance its roundness and warmth to the detriment of its distinctive freshness. On the contrary, serving an excessively cold red wine can hide its main gustatory traits by intensifying its hard parts – particularly its tannic texture. It is also worth keeping in mind that all wines, especially if drunk in warm environments such as the kitchen, tend to warm up quite quickly once in the glass. That is why the practice of cooling down even the most ambitious red wines for a few minutes in the fridge shouldn't be regarded with suspicion, as they will reach their ideal temperature just a few minutes after serving. Furthermore many red wines are erroneously served at the famous "room temperature" which can irreparably compromise the tasting, especially in summer. A very useful tool is the glacette, a container filled with water and ice for around 2/3 of its capacity, which can cool down a warm wine in a few minutes.

The following are guidelines worth considering along with that which has already been said; it is always better for the wine to be cooler rather than too warm.

✎ 06/08°C – Sparkling wines made with the Charmat method, both dry and sweet

✎ 08/10°C – Young and thin bodied white wines, "sur lie" white wines, sparkling wines made with the Champenoise (or classic) method

✎ 10/12°C – Medium bodied white wines, young and thin bodied rose wines, particularly rich sparkling wines made with the Champenoise method

✎ 12/14°C – Full bodied rose wines, white passito and liquoroso

✎ 14/16°C – Young and thin bodied red wines, red passito and liquoroso

✎ 16/18°C – Medium bodied red wines

✎ 18/20°C – Full bodied red wines, especially if aged

THE MANAGEMENT OF THE CELLAR

Whether big or small, a good cellar generally needs to have 3 important characteristics, those ideal for the perfect storage of its precious bottles.

For example nothing interferes with wine more than light exposure, either natural or artificial. That is why a good cellar must be windowless; a place where direct daylight can't filter through. One of the reasons why cellars are usually located underground has also to do with temperature changes; the best cellars boast a rather stable average temperature, not too cold in winter and most importantly not too hot in summer. There are many schools of thought on the subject and a minimum temperature variation has recently been considered as positive, for it allows the wine to "breathe", this way letting it evolve and develop slowly but consistently. Without worrying too much about minor exceptions, the reference temperature is between 13/14 and 17/18°C. Also the bottles are kept positioned horizontally for a specific reason: this way the cork is always in contact with the liquid without drying too much and therefore preventing unpleasant and premature oxidations. That is why the ideal cellar needs to have a certain amount of humidity; however in case it is too strong, it can help to wrap the bottles in common kitchen film, in order not to ruin the labels. It is also preferable if the cellar is in a place with no intense odors – cheese and cold meat are usually left to age in separate chambers – and the least amount of vibrations – for instance due to proximity to trains and the underground.

These are general guidelines, which are valid especially for those bottles whose resting period in the cellar is going to last many years. In the opposite case, if they will be consumed within a few months, these simple rules tend to count less and any place in the house can be suitable for storage.

THE BUBBLES AND THE MAGIC
OF SPARKLING WINES

The bubbles rise buoyantly out of the glass and with them comes the sensation of partaking in something magical, as if that wine was able to capture a rare purity, as an evocation of ancient wisdom. However sparkling wine is relatively young; its birth is strictly connected to the invention of glass and to the increasing popularity of cork. These two materials are fundamental to create what had been impossible beforehand, i.e. the re-fermentation of wine in a bottle to create those bubbles that are nowadays always associated with parties and celebrations.

They are wines with an infinite variety of nuances, not only of color: from extremely light colored to more intense ones recalling golden hues, or rosé ones and even some rare reds. They are all capable to delight with an impressive wide olfactory range. It is not rare to come across strong floral notes, more or less warm, that fade into fruity scents – citrus as well as fruit of white, yellow and red pulp. All these scents are strictly linked to the varietals used for the production of the wine. Within the traditional method – used for the production of the most important and illustrious sparkling wines in the world, such as Champagne – a common trait is represented by the olfactory notes resulting from the secondary fermentation: bread crust, yeasted dough, marzipan and pan brioche as well as patisserie and honey. Once inside the bottle, they are able to develop and evolve in a distinctive way. However they are not all the same: the popular Prosecco is for instance produced following a completely different technique that allows the wine to develop fresher, more fragrant scents once in the bottle, enjoyable for their immediate freshness.

Although being widely popular all over the world in any location where vineyards have been planted, only a few regions are able to produce unmistakably classy, graceful and long lived sparkling wines. Above all is the already mentioned Champagne; however the entire country is famous for the production of a great number of excellent Crémants, from the Loire Valley to Burgundy, Alsace and beyond. Beyond French borders, sparkling wine takes on different names, often in connection with the area of production: just to mention the most popular, Franciacorta in Italy and Cava in Spain. Their gastronomic function is not limited to being drunk as an aperitif. Quite the contrary; thanks to their structure, some sparkling wines are capable to be the perfect company for any type of dish, from the simplest to the richest. Their charming nature makes people look at them with curiosity and admiration. Well, we just need to pop a bottle then!

CHAMPAGNE
LET'S PARTY!

Bubbles, bubbles, bubbles. There is no other wine in the world as famous and popular as Champagne, the father of all sparkling wines. Boasting a rich history and unique territory, it is able to surprise and amaze as only few other wines can, fueling its own myth.

The narrative goes back centuries: despite the cultivation of grapes in the Champagne area dating back to the Roman domain, it was only in the 16th century that the area became popular for the production of a wine known as "vin gris" (grey wine), after the rosy color resulting from the vinification of Pinot Noir, Pinot Meunier and Chardonnay varietals, without contact with the skins. At that time it was not unusual that wines couldn't complete their fermentation, especially because of the cold winters, and so they had to be sent out when still slightly sweet. With the temperatures increasing in spring, it could therefore happen that they started to develop the carbonation typical of sparkling wines, whilst still in bottle. However, the Champagne that we are familiar with today was born in the 1700s due to the increasing popularity of glass bottles and corks; as fundamental requirements for a second more or less controlled fermentation, they also allowed the experimentation of the first attempts of Cuvée, i.e. blending wines of different origins with the purpose of obtaining the best possible result. These practices improved and became more and more popular over the centuries. Thanks to the fundamental support of the first maisons, Champagne has seen a constant and consistent technical improvement that has led it to become what we know it as today: the best sparkling wine in the world. The results of research and studies developed over the centuries are today replicated in almost all wine making areas under the name of "Classic Method" (or Méthode Champenoise, after the name of the region). France can boast excellent sparkling wines under the name of Crémant, in areas such as the Loire, Burgundy and Alsatian, to quote just a few.

The region of Champagne, situated about 150 km north-east of Paris, has however shown what excellent sparkling wines its grapes can deliver. It is a territory that can boast a unique sum of factors – from the climate to the soil – which are unequaled anywhere else.

As a varietal suitable for producing sparkling wines all over the world, Chardonnay best expresses itself in the Champagne area known as Côte des Blancs.

A unique peculiarity of the Champagne region is the millions years old subsoil: a mix of limestone and gypsum, able to retain the winter and spring rains and to constantly release moisture during the drier months. That is not all: the same action occurs with the summer warmth that keeps the plants alive during winter. The Champagne region is unique for many other reasons: for example, it is the northernmost region in Europe where it is possible to produce high quality wines (with the rising temperatures, it has recently started to be possible in England too). Over the centuries, thanks to the virtuous human contribution, the region has been able to select what are now considered the most traditional wine varietals for the production of Champagne. Those varietals – Pinot Noir, Pinot Meunier and Chardonnay – have managed to adapt over time to the unique characteristics of the area, improving their quality in a slow and consistent way. They are the base of Champagne.

The label on the bottle is of great help in understanding many things about its Champagne content. A Blanc de Blancs is, for instance, always produced solely from Chardonnay grapes. A Blanc de Noirs, on the contrary, comes solely from black grapes: Pinot Noir and/or Pinot Meunier. In the entire region the former is more popular, for being easier to cultivate and to age, but definitely less talented in terms of fineness and elegance.

The vast majority of Champagnes for sale every year are bottled as Sans Année (SA – without year, or non-vintage, NV), meaning that they are the result of a blend of wines from different vintages. In order to offer wines that are able to express themselves in the same way with minimal differences from year to year, all the major maisons keep a substantial quantity of wine in their cellars, known as "reserve" wines. These wines are normally used in a percentage of 10/20% along with the liqueur de dosage (a mixture of wine with a small amount of sugar), with the purpose of delivering that unique timbre that distinguishes one maison from another. More than any other region in the world, Champagne is the birthplace of the intergenerational Cuvée: the art of wisely fusing several types of wine coming from different years. In charge of this delicate operation is the Chef de Cave, who has to make sure that the quality of the final product is superior to the sum of the single wines combined to make it. This process is anything but simple, with dozens of ever-changing variables: from the climate of the previous year to the peculiarities of each vineyard or to the different areas of origin. If a Champagne is not the result of a fusion but comes from just one harvest, then it is defined and labeled as Millesimato. In most cases this translates into the most prestigious and ambitious Champagne.

Moreover, the role played by sugar is also crucial to better understanding the information on the package. The driest Champagnes are the ones that are not "sweetened" during the production process: they are called Brut Nature (or Pas Dosé and Dosage Zerò, a category growing in popularity). Quite similar, except for a slightly higher sugar content, are the Extra-Bruts. These are followed by the appreciated and popular category of Brut, by far the most common. The other categories are Extra Sec or Extra Dry, Sec or Dry, Demi-Sec and finally Doux, sweet Champagnes often with great charm.

Finally, the label contains the initials that identify the production structure behind the Champagne. The most common are NM, RM, CM. The first stands for Négociant Manipulant and refers to those maisons or wine makers who buy their grapes supplies from third parties in order to make their own wines. In the Champagne region there is a long familiar tradition of provision, as a real source for a large number of wineries. The second category, which has seen a growth in recent decades, stands for Récoltant Manipulant, i.e. wine makers whose production exclusively comes from their own grapes. The third category, the Coopérative de Manipulation, recalls the great French tradition of the social wineries, which process and sell the grapes of their own associates.

Overall it is a unique territory where big maisons and small vignerons give their contribution to maintaining the myth of Champagne alive, harvest after harvest; a wine that more than any other is synonymous with partying, thanks also to the multiple art masterpieces that have celebrated it.

TYPE: *sparkling white, dry*

COLOR: *straw-yellow, with extremely fine and persistent bubbles*

BOUQUET: *intense, pure, floral and fruity, with mineral and citrus notes and subtle hints of bread crust and small patisserie*

TASTING NOTE: *more or less dry depending on the sugar residues, dry or rounded, full, harmonious and with great persistence*

VARIETAL: *Chardonnay, Pinot Noir, Pinot Meunier*

DENOMINATION: *Champagne AOC (Appellation of Controlled Origin)*

REGION: *Champagne, France*

SERVING TEMPERATURE: *7/9°C*

MINIMUM ALCOHOL CONTENT: *10.5%*

PAIRING: *starters from the sea – crustaceans, raw fish, mixed tempuras – as well as risotto, pies and other main courses from the land*

PROSECCO
ITALIAN BUBBLES

The world famous Italian sparkling wine, a business worth 400 million bottles each year, has an ancient yet young history: *"And now I would like to wet my mouth with that Prosecco with its apple bouquet"* wrote Aureliano Acanti in 1754. During the Roman era, grapes that were initially cultivated in the village of Prosecco, on the Carso hills near Trieste, were used to produce a wine called Puccino. In the 13th century Glera – the white grape varietal which is at the core of Prosecco – became extensively popular all over the hills of Veneto and Friuli; it is at that time that it imposed itself as one of the most common and appreciated varietals. The real change and great productive push came in the 1900s with the introduction of new technologies for the making of sparkling wine; Prosecco began to populate tables all over the world, quickly becoming protagonist of the great phenomenon we know today.

The production of Prosecco involves a vast area, including several provinces and two entire regions: a land that begins in Vicenza, Veneto, and ends in Trieste, Friuli-Venezia Giulia, therefore embracing the largest part of north east Italy. In this vast area, a well-defined territory is considered to be the heart of the production, 50 km from Venice, it is a hilly strip of land that starts in Asolo and ends in Conegliano. Between the two towns is the municipality considered to be the most influential in the production of Prosecco: Valdobbiadene. This area is at an equal distance between the Alps and the Adriatic Sea, with an ideal climatic combination; in its extremely steep and hard to cultivate hills, the Glera grape finds the perfect conditions to express itself at its highest potential. Here some of the most interesting sparkling wines of the whole denomination are produced: Prosecco wines with vitality, dynamism and more in general purity, qualities that are simply impossible to find anywhere else. Moreover, within the same area of Valdobbiadene, is a hill which is considered to be the quality apex of that pyramid that makes the world of Prosecco: a special place, where the grapes reach perfect ripening with unique balance. It is called Cartizze and many wine producers are proud to mention it on their labels.

The development of the Prosecco we know today, quantity and quality wise, would have never been possible without the fundamental contribution of one of the most prestigious enological schools in Italy, the first founded in the country: Conegliano. Its rooms have seen different generations thriving to contribute to the constant improvement of the production process, from the cultivation of the grapes up to each phase of the wine making procedure.

TYPE: sparkling white wine, dry

COLOR: light straw yellow, with rather fine and persistent bubbles

BOUQUET: fragrant, with notes of fresh fruit – apple, pear and citrus – blending into floral scents

TASTING NOTE: fresh, dry and rich with floral hints

VARIETAL: Glera

DENOMINATION: Conegliano Valdobbiadene Prosecco DOCG (Denomination of Controlled and Guaranteed Origin), Asolo Prosecco DOCG, Prosecco DOC (Denomination of Controlled Origin)

REGION: Veneto and Friuli-Venezia Giulia, Italy

SERVING TEMPERATURE: 5/7°C

MINIMUM ALCOHOL CONTENT: 9%

PAIRING: vegetarian cuisine and starters from the land – legumes soups and mild cheese in particular

Today, after the harvest and first vinification, the result is what is called basic wine, which after a brief resting period in the cellar is assembled and placed inside stainless steel tanks, typical of the area of Prosecco. In these huge stainless steel pressure containers the wine can ferment along with the sugar and the yeast, to produce those familiar bubbles. This method, known under the name of its inventor Martinotti, consists of a brief phase of secondary fermentation in stainless steel tanks for no longer than 30 days. Just to make a comparison, let's think that in the Classic Method – or Méthode Champenoise, used for the production of Champagne – the transformation by the yeast of the sugar into alcohol and in carbon dioxide happens in the bottle and it can last many, many months. In the last few years some wine producers have recovered an old production methodology: the Prosecco being re-fermented in the bottle, as per the farming tradition which is still alive in a big part of the denomination. This is a slightly cloudy sparkling wine with a sure gastronomical vocation, called "sur lie" or "on the lees".

Not all Proseccos are the same; they differentiate for the production area but also, and foremost, for their sugar residue. Prosecco Brut is the driest and the type that has grown the most in terms of consumers' appreciation in the last few years. Prosecco Extra Dry is the traditional one, relatively dry and with an unmistakable softness that makes it extremely pleasant and suitable for any occasion. Prosecco Dry is the least common and at the same time the one that tends to be the most amiable, slightly sweet, perfect to wrap up a good dinner with. In all cases, Prosecco has shown a unique flexibility in the last decades; a sparkling wine unique for its fragrance and balance, as easy to drink as it is rich in tradition and history.

In some of the areas where Prosecco is produced, it is common that the organoleptic profile of the wines is strongly affected by gypsum sediment.

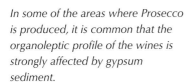

THE BEAUTY AND HARMONY OF WHITE WINES

The concept of white wine comprises an incredible variety of colors, fragrances, tastes, production styles and geographical areas. If taken together, these characteristics compose an extraordinarily fascinating landscape; possessing a key to ever diversified interpretations, they are capable of revealing a surprisingly complex gustatory range upon tasting. Whether dark and tending to amber, golden or even very pale, each white wine is a discovery of the roots that connect it to the history of its region of production. White wine, as a synonym of wine itself, has been walking alongside mankind for over 2000 years, loyally shadowing through migrations and conquests by adapting to diverse climatic conditions, even to those very different from its land of origin. Thanks to this long adaptation process, it is today possible to talk about Chardonnay in France or Riesling in Germany. Both varietals have managed to perfectly readjust to specific places through the centuries and, along with the patient human effort, to deliver wines that it is not possible to replicate anywhere else. Unique wines.

By looking at the world map, it is fascinating to see just how well white wines are able to express themselves in different ways at different latitudes. Some of the most elegant and long lived white wines come from northern regions – Loire, Burgundy or Mosel – at the same time those coming from the south are equally extraordinary – the wine from Irpinia, Italy, just to mention one. What associates all great white wines is their ability to amplify their virtues with the passing of time; they challenge the seasons and are able to delight even after many years. Whether they are aged in steel tanks, in barrels or even inside urns, what remains after many years is the human ability to exploit their innermost nature, to enhance the natural characteristics and thereby produce wines with guaranteed charm.

They are extraordinarily eclectic wines, suitable for any moment during the day as well as during any type of meal; this central feature helps to understand their wide popularity in any land where the grapes have managed to find the right conditions to survive. Such a diversity is reflected in a stunningly beautiful enological landscape, to be discovered glass after glass, year after year. It is certainly time well invested.

Geographically closer to the area of Champagne than to Burgundy or other wine making regions, Chablis is one of the symbolic territories for French wine. Here some of the most acclaimed Chardonnay-based white wines of the world are produced; their mineral complexity, elegance and longevity are practically impossible to reproduce anywhere else.

Chablis is not only the name of the wine but also of a small town in the northernmost part of the Burgundy region, north-west of the Côte de Nuits and southeast of Paris; the town is around 200 km from the capital and has always been an important reference for both red and white wines. However, with the development of other communication routes and, above all, with the arrival of the Phylloxera epidemic in the second half of the 1800s, the area was afflicted by a long period of crisis and the consequent mass abandonment of the countryside. This period culminated in the Second World War. Just to give an idea, the production of white wine was down to just 481 hectoliters in 1945 compared to the 15,000 hectoliters in 1938. In the following years the fame of Chablis progressively returned to its splendor, new vineyards were planted and new wineries were built: it was impossible to forget the unique purity of the white wines from this area.

The origin of such elegance can be found in the calcareous and rich fossil soils, as much as in the climatic conditions: the cool weather is ideal for the production of wines which are never too warm and always carry a well-balanced freshness. One of the biggest threats for the local wine makers are sudden spring frosts; such occurrences can be overcome either by heating the air in the vineyards with huge stoves or by wetting the plants. External-only ice is able to protect the grapes from the cold.

The classification of Chablis wines perfectly represents the importance of the soil as well as of the climate, especially in the northernmost regions. All Grand Cru vineyards in fact face south and south-west, where there are the perfect conditions for a perfect ripening of the Chardonnay. There are 7 in total – Vaudésir, Blanchot, Bougros, Les Clos, Grenouilles, Les Preuses, Valmur – and they are all situated on the hills overlooking the town of Chablis. At the heart of these beautiful plots is also La Moutonne, a plot of roughly 2 hectares that is not part of the official denomination and is bottled as such by one sole winery; a unique case for the entire area under "monopoly".

CHABLIS
THE UNREACHABLE PURITY OF NORTHERN WHITES

In the quality pyramid of Chablis wines the next step is represented by the Premier Cru wines, immediately followed by Chablis, by far the most common type, and finally Petit-Chablis, a separate denomination of minor qualitative importance.

Chablis wines have been long considered synonymous with "dry whites", i.e. wines that break away from those soft traits that had been so popular in a large part of the enological world particularly at the end of the 20th century. They can surprise with their strong minerality, reminiscent of gunflint, and pleasant scents of wild flowers and citrus. However it is in the mouth that great Chablis wines really distance themselves from other Chardonnay-based whites from other areas of the world: they are extraordinarily complex, characterized by a vehement acidity, multi-faceted and easy to drink at the same time. A vertical expression of an overall grand harmony.

TYPE: white, dry
COLOR: light straw-yellow
BOUQUET: ample and very refined with notes of green apple, cedar, lemon, lime wood, gypsum, butter, vanilla, hazelnuts
TASTING NOTE: fresh, with good acidity, definite complexity and persistence
VARIETAL: Chardonnay
DENOMINATION: Chablis AOC (Appellation of Controlled Origin)
REGION: Burgundy, France
SERVING TEMPERATURE: 8/10°C
MINIMUM ALCOHOL CONTENT: 10%
PAIRING: starters and main courses from the sea – oysters, crustaceans, white meat and steamed vegetables in particular

CHÂTEAU-CHALON
THE BEAUTY OF OXIDATION

Small quantities of confident originality: that's how we can summarize some of those wines produced in the stunning region of Jura, in central-eastern France, not far from the more well-known Burgundy. Despite its size, Jura offers a particularly varied selection of white and red wines, which include the varietals of Pinot Noir but as well as the more local Poulsard, fresher and fruitier, and Trousseau, warmer and deeper. It is however for whites that Jura is famous in the world. They are divided in two large categories: the ones produced in a traditional way, like in other parts of the country, and the oxidatively aged ones, i.e. intentionally left in contact with the air. This latter practice is typical of the entire region and it makes it stand out in the landscape of wines; not only the French ones.

Vin Jaune, literally "yellow wine", is the most famous. The Sauvignon grapes used for the production are picked when fully ripe, then vinificated and consequently left to age for a very long period of time in wooden barrels, which are intentionally emptied for a third of their capacity. These containers can even be very old and are usually slightly bigger than the more common Barriques – 228 liters – often built using oak from the surrounding woods. In such a unique context, the wine is never mixed with the Bâtonnage technique and so the surface of the liquid gets covered by a thin film of yeasts that protect the wine from a dangerous vinegary drift. This veil, voile in French, can guarantee a perfect environment to protect the wine for a period up to 6 years long. That is how the wine manages to evolve and to express, once in the bottle, a robust and original organoleptic profile; its olfactory range includes peanuts, hazelnuts and more in general dried fruits, acacia honey, hay and musk, up to hints of mushrooms. Furthermore, Vin Jaune gives out unique sensations upon tasting: dry, with a special balance that conveys a gustatory fulfillment, capable of blending structure and persistence within a context of great freshness.

Although popular throughout the entire region, only within the boundaries of the municipality of Château-Chalon can Vin Jaune take the name of the location, where it is possible to find some of the most celebrated wines of Jura. Those fifty hectares deliver wines of great substance and longevity, which evolve in the bottle for decades without seeing their depth fading over time. Unforgettable wines.

Both Vin Jaune and Château-Chalon wines are traditionally sold inside a specifically designed bottle, the so-called Clavelin, which has a capacity of 62cl, instead of 75cl. There is a reason for that: during its extremely long aging process, it is estimated that each liter of wine loses slightly less than 40% of its volume, by dispersion in the cellar air. Each bottle therefore represents what is left to the wine maker of that initial liter.

TYPE: *white, dry*

COLOR: *light golden yellow*

BOUQUET: *intense and deep with notes of dried fruits, hay, algae, acacia, humus and vanilla*

TASTING NOTE: *very dry, captivating, sustained by a robust acidity and great persistence*

VARIETAL: *Savagnin*

DENOMINATION: *Château-Chalon AOC (Appellation of Controlled Origin)*

REGION: *Jura*

SERVING TEMPERATURE: *10/12°C*

MINIMUM ALCOHOL CONTENT: *12%*

PAIRING: *courses from the land – aged cheese in particular*

FIANO DI AVELLINO
AN ABUNDANCE OF ELEGANCE IN IRPINIA

One of the best Italian wines comes from Campania, and more specifically from the heart of the province of Avellino. Far from any possible stereotype about southern Italy, Irpinia is characterized by an almost continental climate: the average temperatures are amongst the lowest of the region and abundant rains rage throughout the four seasons. It is therefore no coincidence that the white wines from this area are anything but warm, being much closer to some French wines than to their Campanian "brothers". Moreover, the whole of Irpinia has in the last decades been somehow left out from the development of the main transport networks in the south of Italy, roads in particular. This has meant that the whole area has over time maintained a strong bond with its traditions, especially those related to agriculture. It has been an extremely difficult process: let's just say that for a good part of the past century, decade after decade, the area saw its countryside progressively abandoned in favor of cultivating non-native varietals, believed to be more resistant and productive. Hence, if today it is possible to talk about a true rebirth of Fiano di Avellino it is only thanks to those sparse entities that have guaranteed its survival throughout the years, strongly believing in their own uniqueness and character. It is indeed a special white, which can express itself with a purity and energy which are rarely found in other wines, at least not in Italy. It gives its best when processed in those widely popular steel containers, which can influence its character so markedly. That is how it manages to maintain its fragrance and its gentle minerality, specific to its younger phase. However it is only a matter of time: with aging, the best Fiano di Avellino wines come up with smoky, iodized notes and scents of hydrocarbon. This is another element of unique charm and complexity that places Fiano di Avellino not only amongst the most long-lived, but also as one of the best Italian white wines for its nuances and elegance.

TYPE: *white, dry*

COLOR: *straw-yellow*

BOUQUET: *sharp and pure, with notes of yellow flowers, lemon and citrus in general, almond, hazelnut, chestnut flour, sea salt, gypsum*

TASTING NOTE: *fresh, rich, well balanced between acidity and sapidity*

VARIETAL: *Fiano*

DENOMINATION: *Fiano di Avellino DOCG (Denomination of Controlled and Guaranteed Origin)*

REGION: *Campania, Italy*

SERVING TEMPERATURE: *8/10°C*

MINIMUM ALCOHOL CONTENT: *11%*

PAIRING: *main courses from the land and the sea – soups, char-grilled fish, pizza and focaccia in particular*

MONTRACHET
THE GLORY OF GREAT FRENCH WINES

As the birthplace of some of the world's greatest wines, in the collective imagination Burgundy represents the perfect fusion of history, vocation of the area, talented varietals and workmanship. It is a rather vast territory that stretches from Lion to Dijon, without including the area of Chablis which is more to the north-west. Here the Chardonnay and Pinot Noir grapes can perform at their best by delivering wines of incomparable elegance and longevity. From Beaujolais – home to Gamay – to the area of Mâconnais, from the Côte Chalonnaise to the Côte d'Or (then divided into the Côte de Beaune and the Côte de Nuits) there are a multitude of denominations – almost 100 – and famous wineries. However overall they are small entities; the average extension of each vineyard in the whole region is only slightly above 7 hectares. Such a territorial fragmentation is the distinctive world-renowned trait of Burgundy; its vineyards are often cultivated, vinificated and then commercialized by several *domaines*, representing a unique peculiarity that makes one appreciate the diverse nuances of its wines.

In addition Burgundy can boast an inimitable wine classification, the best expression of which can be found in the Côte d'Or. The easiest and wider spread wines have the region as their focal strong point. Their labels bear *Bourgogne Rouge* or *Bourgogne Blanc*, which identify red and white wines often produced from grapes coming from different municipalities. The most important are the so called *Village* wines, which are produced within the borders of a specific municipality, which appears on the label. Some of them are extremely famous: Puligny-Montrachet, Aloxe-Corton, Nuits-St.-Georges, Vosne-Romanée etc. The next step is represented by those wines that have a single vineyard as a protagonist, i.e. all grapes used to produce a single bottle come from there. Over the centuries, Burgundy has divided its best territories into 2 categories; *Premier Cru* and *Grand Cru* where unique vineyards simply express the highest level of perfection the territory can reach and offer. The *Premier Crus* are over 500 and correspond to around 10% of the regional production. On the label they are always indicated after the name of the municipality they belong to. The *Grand Crus* are around 33, therefore reaching barely the 2% of the regional production, and their fame is such that they don't need further geographical information aside.

Thanks to specific geological characteristics – the entire Côte d'Or sits alongside an important limestone-based geological fault – and to the perfect location, facing east/south-east, these vineyards deliver wines which are always different from one another, but not less excellent in their respective forms: they are unique, pure, rich in details, energetic and long-lived.

Amongst the white wines, possibly the most important is Montrachet: a *Grand Cru* of around 8 hectares, half way between Chassagne-Montrachet and Puligny-Montrachet, in the heart of the Côte de Beaune. It is surrounded by 4 neighboring vineyards that are still part of the *Grand Cru*: Chevalier-Montrachet, Bâtard-Montrachet, Bienvenues-Bâtard-Montrachet and Criots-Bâtard-Montrachet. Here the Chardonnay is able to fully develop its complexity and therefore produce some of the most intense, rich and strong white wines in the world. They are almost always left to age in 228-liter Barriques, which are often subjected to the *Bâtonnage* technique: the wine is periodically stirred with a baton in order to mix and bring back to surface the lees that had been sedimented at the bottom. This way the wine acquires more body and more aromas. A classic Montrachet features beautiful golden nuances that anticipate an enthralling olfactory profile: notes of apple and hawthorn along with scents of butter, oriental spices, acacia honey and dried fruits. On top of that are constant mineral references which are perceptible in the mouth as well. Ample, intense, deep yet energetic, fresh and persistent at the same time, these wines can delight even after a very long time. Their consumption is always recommended from at least 10 years after the harvest. Despite their exorbitant cost, they are worth tasting at least once in a lifetime.

TYPE: white, dry
COLOR: light golden yellow
BOUQUET: ample, deep with notes of hawthorn, ripe grapes, lemon grass, marzipan, hazelnuts, green apple, butter, croissant, gypsum, acacia honey
TASTING NOTE: full, soft, with a decisive freshness and extraordinary harmony
VARIETAL: Chardonnay
DENOMINATION: Puligny-Montrachet AOC (Appellation of Controlled Origin)
REGION: Burgundy, France
SERVING TEMPERATURE: 9/11°C
MINIMUM ALCOHOL CONTENT: 12%
PAIRING: main courses from the land and the sea – oven-baked fish and white meat in particular – and crustacean starters

MÜLLER THURGAU
AROMA AND ELEGANCE

Less intense than the famous Gewürztraminer, Müller Thurgau has over time managed to find its way into the favor of many enthusiasts thanks to its subtle sapidity. Along with natural primary scents of apple, pear, lime, broom and sage, its delicate savory touch makes it a particularly elegant wine, suitable for pairing with the most diversified food on the most diversified occasions.

The white wine comes from the namesake varietal, which was created artificially in 1882 by Hermann Müller, a Swiss botanist from the Canton of Thurgau. That is how it acquired its name. Between the middle and end of the 1800s, a large number of scientists put their efforts into combining different varietals sometimes very different from one another. The purpose was always the same: to harness the peculiarities of each varietal in order to generate a new different one that would combine the qualities of all the singles. In the case of Müller Thurgau, the first varietal was Riesling, which is the foundation of many complex, intense and pure wines.

The second varietal, on the other hand, has always been source of doubt: it was initially thought to be Silvaner, very popular in Alsace, France, and in some areas of Germany, much appreciated for its premature ripening. However recent studies seem to suggest that it could be either the more common Chasselas – which over time has spread into central European countries – or the rarer Madeleine Royale. What is certain is that the result of the fusion had an extraordinary success; from the 100-150 plants that Hermann Müller created experimentally in Switzerland, the varietal became the most popular in Germany by 1970. One of the reasons of such success is surely to be found in its great capability to adapt to the most disparate soils and climates and in its great vigor: the latter has been long considered the central characteristic.

Things have changed significantly nowadays: although Müller Thurgau is still extremely popular in the regions of Baden, Rhenish Hesse, Franconia and Rhineland-Palatinate, it has also received great appreciation in Austria, Italy, Hungary and the Czech Republic, followed by minor impact in England and Switzerland. It can be vinificated both as sweet and as sparkling version, with excellent results. It is however in its traditional dry white version that it can offer the best sensations: a gracious and aromatic olfactory spectrum combined with a decisive freshness. All successful ingredients.

TYPE: white, dry
COLOR: intense straw yellow
BOUQUET: pure, with pleasant notes of citrus, apple, pear,
pineapple, mango, ginger and white pepper
TASTING NOTE: elegant, intense, pleasantly sapid and with
good freshness
VARIETAL: Müller Thurgau
DENOMINATION: Rheinterrasse
REGION: Rheinhessen, Germany
SERVING TEMPERATURE: 8/10°C
MINIMUM ALCOHOL CONTENT: 12%
PAIRING: vegetarian and oriental cuisine – minestrone and
soups, white meat and fresh water fish in particular.

*The Pinot Grigio grapes are typically
dark colored, recalling copper.*

PINOT GRIS
ALSATIAN PURITY

Stretching from north to south, from Strasbourg to Mulhouse in the east of France, Alsace is renowned all over the world for its white wine production. Here the different types of grapes are historically vinificated on their own and only rarely are they blended; the purpose is to glorify their unique characteristics. Along with the soil and more in general the *terroir*, those features make Alsatian wines unique within the transalpine landscape. There is a reason for this: as a borderland, Alsace is very close to German wine-making traditions; the well-known area of Baden is only a few km from the adjacent river Rhine. Unlike in Germany though, here white wines are brought to dryness naturally, so it is quite rare to find those "abboccato" versions (i.e. slightly sweet) which are so typical of the Teutonic tradition.

One of the distinctive traits of Alsace within the European context is related to its extraordinary geological fragmentation; a true pastiche that delivers wines with one occasionally being very different from another, although often produced within a few hundred meters apart. Despite this, the original varietal name is always at the center of the bottle label, unlike many other French denominations where the location is the protagonist. The classification offers useful information: the vineyards included in the list of Grand Crus are those capable of offering the best of Alsace, in terms of mineral purity and longevity. These are wines that are produced at the heart of the denomination, in its southernmost part. Their product specification establishes lower yields in the countryside, stricter rules for the vinification phase and above all the use of only the most suitable varietals: Gewürztraminer – in France spelled without the German dieresis – Riesling, White Moscato and Pinot Grigio.

The latter is very popular in the north-east of Italy as well and it is the father of Pinot Gris, one of the most prestigious white wines of the area. Its history dates back centuries: in 1565 the Baron Lazare de Schwendi brought some vine plants from the town of Tokay, in Hungary, back to Alsace. Once in Kientzheim, where his castle is still visible today, he started planting those vines with the purpose of reproducing the famous and exquisite Hungarian sweet wine. However, some ampelographers believe that what he brought back to France didn't correspond to Furmint – the prominent varietal used in Tokaji. They believe it was actually a clone of the already famous Pinot Noir.

Gneiss is an old rock and a crucial geological component of the organoleptic profile of the best Alsatian wines.

Such a linguistic misunderstanding lasted for centuries: before 1870 it was called Grauer Tokayer, then Alsatian Tokay and finally Tokay Pinot Gris. The issue was resolved only in 2007, with an internal European agreement that swept away the customer's confusion.

Like other great Alsatian white wines, Pinot Gris can be produced as *Vendange Tardive* or as *Sélection de Grains Nobles*. The former is a sweet wine with outstanding organoleptic features; the harvest starts a few weeks late, during which the grapes, like for Sauternes wines, get wrapped in a thin film of *Botrytis Cinerea* mold, which later on contributes to the gustatory profile in vinification. The same can be said for the latter, although it is the result of an even more accurate selection of the grapes during the harvest. Only the best and those considered perfect, are going to form that nectar which

possesses a rare charming softness and complexity and is capable of competing against some of the best sweet wines worldwide.

Nevertheless, the most popular Pinot Gris is the dry version, a white wine with gorgeous golden nuances that recall the coppery coloring of its grapes, with an extremely complex and enthralling aromatic component; apricot and other dried fruit, honey, beeswax combine with smoky scents that recall the undergrowth – musk, mushrooms and lichens in particular. In its best interpretations, it is a rounded white with a softness perfectly balanced by decisive freshness and subtle minerality, subsequently acquiring an exquisite gustatory profile that announces a long persistence on the finish. A great French white.

TYPE: white, dry

COLOR: intense straw yellow, often tending to amber

BOUQUET: full and elegant, with notes of lemon, lime, pear, apple, orange peel, acacia honey and with precious mineral hints

TASTING NOTE: very fresh, soft, rich, with good acidity and persistence

VARIETAL: Pinot Grigio

DENOMINATION: Alsace AOC (Appellation of Controlled Origin)

REGION: Alsace, France

SERVING TEMPERATURE: 8/10°C

MINIMUM ALCOHOL CONTENT: 10%

PAIRING: vegetarian cuisine and courses from the sea – rich mixed salads and grilled fish in particular

POUILLY-FUMÉ
THE INIMITABLE AROMAS OF SAUVIGNON BLANC

Some of the most important white wines in the whole of France come from the easternmost tip of the Loire Valley: Sancerre, on the left bank of the river, and a few km south on the right bank, Pouilly-sur-Loire. These unique wines emanate special aromas that remain impressed on the memory once tasted: they can sweep you away with essences that recall nettle leaves and green pepper, as well as fruity notes of pineapple, cedar, lychee and passion fruit. Their olfactory profile is enriched by floral traces of acacia as well as spicy ones – white pepper, minerals and gun flint. These are only a few of the most recognizable traits, which can develop in multiple nuances all anticipating a fresh tasting, during which the acidity is perfectly balanced by good body and decisive persistence.

The scents and characteristics undoubtedly all point towards a varietal that only in this area can express its personality and elegance: Sauvignon Blanc. Famous and widely spread from New Zealand – where it is the base of some great white wines – to South Africa, Chile and the United States, practically every country offers the possibility to find close to exact versions of it. Originally from Bordeaux, this varietal is considered one of the most important worldwide for the quantity and the quality of the wines that it generates.

The area of Sancerre is quite vast and includes several municipalities; the area where Pouilly-Fumé is produced is slightly smaller and includes only those towns bordering the namesake one. This difference reflects on the hectares dedicated to vineyards: almost 3000 in the former case, less than 1500 in the latter. However these differences almost disappear in the glass; in their best versions, both wines are particularly elegant, complex, with good longevity and a magnificent balance of all their components.

In the Loire Valley many cellars are built by carving out the tuff, a rock widely diffused in the area.

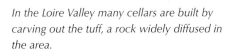

However the name Pouilly-Fumé itself suggests a peculiarity that is not possible to find anywhere else: thanks to the strong presence of silicon and other minerals in the soils where the Sauvignon Blanc varietal is cultivated, the wine acquires certain slightly smoky notes that recall gun flint and, more in general, strong mineral scents. A very magnetic and unforgettable trait indeed.

TYPE: white, dry
COLOR: straw-yellow
BOUQUET: intense and subtle with notes of nettle, green pepper, grapefruit, lychee, pineapple, passion fruit, acacia, vanilla and white pepper
TASTING NOTE: resh, linear, elegant and with a marked acidity and great persistence
VARIETAL: Sauvignon Blanc
DENOMINATION: Pouilly-Fumé AOC (Appellation of Controlled Origin)
REGION: Loire Valley, France
SERVING TEMPERATURE: 8/10°C
MINIMUM ALCOHOL CONTENT: 11%
PAIRING: vegetarian cuisine, seafood starters, oven-baked fish, vegetable soups and pureed soups

RIESLING
THE BRIGHTEST WHITE OF ALL

If there was a classification of the most important wine varietals regardless of their popularity, it couldn't fail to include Riesling, a varietal that is able to deliver some of the most vibrant and long-lived white wines in the world. These wines are always characterized by an extraordinary territorial adherence that tells in detail the story of the land where they are born. Such an adherence relates to the latitude as well as to the climate and the soils where the varietal is cultivated.

Although widespread basically all around the world – Austria, Czech Republic, Australia, New Zealand, Canada, the United States and many more – only in Germany and the French region of Alsace it can express its full potential, by even delivering excellent sweet and sparkling wines. In these areas it can stand out in all its purity and particular balance, suspended – especially in Germany – in the perfect fusion of a certain sugar residue and pronounced acidity. An exaggerated freshness would make the wine excessively sterile, whereas a pinch of sugar contributes to making the wine softer, more rounded and deeper. The *Prädikatswein* – the national classification that includes the wines in which it is not possible to add sugar artificially – divides the wines into categories based on the level of aging of the grapes at the moment of harvesting. *Kabinett* wines are the lightest ones, whose grapes are the first to be harvested. *Spätlese* wines (literally: late harvest) are more intense and often slightly sweet. *Auslese* wines, on the other hand, are frequently synonymous with great white wines; their grapes are hand-picked after a first phase during which only the best clusters are selected. *Beerenausleses* are quite rare sweet wines whose grapes are wrapped in the so-called "noble rot". The same happens to the precious *Trockenbeerenauslese* wines, whose grapes have been picked very late, after having lost most part of their weight. Alongside these are the *Eisweins* – or ice wines – whose grapes are picked when still frozen after a frost, so that the aromas and sugars are more concentrated. These indications become useful to understand which wine to expect and they are always accompanied by other indications about the area of origin and residual sweetness – for example, *trocken* means dry.

Although Germany can't compete with France, Italy and Spain from a numerical point of view, some of its famous wine regions deliver some of the most elegant white wines worldwide and that's why Riesling can show its impact.

They are wines usually faded in color but at the same time characterized by an unmistakably charming olfactory profile, with notes of flowers, apple, pear and apricot which blend with strong scents of citrus, cedar, lemon and honey before leaving space to its best and prominent trait: a strong minerality that fades into scents of hydrocarbon, petrol in particular. Once sipped, they stand out for their acidity balanced by a certain sugary roundness, where the sweetest part in the central part of the tasting, fades into an incredibly clean finale.

These small masterpieces frequently originate from the area of Mosella, from the name of the river that runs through the region and characterizes its landscapes. It is in the surrounding areas of Saarburg in particular that the best German white wines are born. Saar – from the name of the tributary of Mosella – is a gorgeous territory, with vineyards dropping sheer to the river and particularly difficult for the grapes which have to literally steal space from the hills in search of the light, vital for their ripening. The whole denomination offers particularly deep wines also further north, in the land of Ruwer or in the surrounding areas of Piesport: beautiful areas, worth visiting at least once.

TYPE: white, dry

COLOR: light straw-yellow

BOUQUET: ample, articulated, with notes of pear, peach, apricot, apple, lemon and honey. Mineral and hydrocarbon scents.

TASTING NOTE: pure, fresh, perfectly balanced between a firm acidity and a subtle sugar residue, with great complexity

VARIETAL: Riesling

DENOMINATION: Mosel

REGION: Mosel, Germany

SERVING TEMPERATURE: 8/10°C

MINIMUM ALCOHOL CONTENT: 7%

PAIRING: vegetarian and oriental cuisine – soups, risotto, white meat and fresh water fish in particular

The geology in Alsace is a true mosaic; however, slate is one of the rocks that most influences the organoleptic profile of the wines produced in the region.

SOAVE
WITH CONSISTENCE AND ELEGANCE

Although misleading when looking at the map, the vast area around Soave is mainly characterized by volcanic soils, which have seen their surrounding geography changing over time; once covered by marine sediments, they come to surface again in the form we know today after corrosive phenomena. These particularly fertile, generous soils give birth to wines of guaranteed complexity and richness.

Hence, it is no coincidence that this territory has always been considered particularly suitable for viticulture. Back during the Roman era, Soave was a district well known for being excellently positioned and intensively cultivated. It was a natural place of trade, well linked to the nearby city of Verona and conveniently situated along the route that crosses a large part of northern Italy. As proof of its viticultural vocation, it is still possible nowadays to read the following inscription on a mural stone in the town center: "As the house of law, erected seventy five years after the year thirteen hundred...when the peasants crush the grapes with their feet". However it was during the 1900s that the fame of Soave wine managed to shift itself beyond the Italian borders; its success brought an increase in production and the creation of a consortium to protect its production in 1926. Moreover, after a few years, in 1931, Soave was recognized, the first amongst Italian wines, as "typical and distinguished".

Produced from the most traditional varietal of the area, Garganega, Soave includes a small percentage of the namesake Trebbiano grape as well. The latter is a varietal that recent studies have proved to be a close relative of Verdicchio, another extremely important Italian varietal. In the attempt to distinguish the most common wines from the ones produced in the most dedicated areas, they created the current denomination of Soave Superiore. The appellation Classico on the label indicates the historical area of production, that one near the municipalities of Soave and Monteforte d'Alpone.

It is a wine of assured elegance characterized by the vastness of its refined scents and by a certain richness. The structure is accompanied by a delicate minerality, a feature that tends to emerge with clarity over the years, after a long period resting in the bottle. Ductile and harmonious, the best wines coming from Soave caress the palate in a succession of unique scents, all ready to be discovered.

TYPE: white, dry
COLOR: intense straw yellow
BOUQUET: pure, with notes of elder and cherry flowers, green apple, peach, pineapple, almond
TASTING NOTE: elegant, rich, slightly bitter and delicately savory
VARIETAL: Garganega, Trebbiano di Soave
DENOMINATION: Soave Superiore DOCG (Denomination of Controlled and Guaranteed origin), Soave DOC (Denomination of Controlled Origin)
REGION: Veneto, Italy
SERVING TEMPERATURE: 9/11°C
MINIMUM ALCOHOL CONTENT: 11%
PAIRING: soups, minestrone, meat-based first courses, white meat

TRAMINER AROMATICO
THOSE OH-SO-CHARMING AROMAS

Mainly known as Gewürztraminer, Traminer Aromatico is produced in Alto Adige and more specifically in the vast area surrounding the town of Termeno. Because of the increasing appreciation it gets, this white wine has over the years managed to spread across the entire provinces of Bolzano and Trento, so much so that it has become one of the most renowned wines of the entire region. Its distinctive trait is to be found in the originality of its olfactory profile and therefore in its intense aroma: scents of rose petals, citrus, exotic fruits and musk. They all go to form a range of attractive aromas, capable of fascinating and enthralling generations of enthusiasts.

The origin of the namesake varietal has been for centuries at the center of a debate, not only in Italy but even in France and Germany. One of the most accredited theories suggests that the Traminer Aromatico varietal was born exactly along the banks of Lake Termeno, or Tramin, from which it takes its name. The first to identify it as such would be the German ampelographer Hermann Goethe, who published his masterpiece Ampelographisches Worterbuch in 1876 – General Ampelographic Catalogue – a true milestone for the subject. However it was only in the following year, 1877, that his Essay of universal ampelography was published with a foreword by Count Giuseppe di Rovasenda, an eclectic character who gathered an enormous amount of notes and minutes on hundreds of varietals. It is in his work that for the first time he states that the origin of Traminer Aromatico is to be found in Alsace; this theory was strongly supported by another important ampelographer of the time, Pierre Galet. For example it is no coincidence that in the nearby region of Jura, the local Savagnin varietal possesses many features similar to Traminer Aromatico.

That's not all: other experts believe it could have been born in the Rhine valley, in Germany. In the area around the middle of the 1800s, it was possible to come across this varietal with its small and compact strawberry blond grapes.

What is certain is that the varietal can deliver assuredly deep, soft and captivating wines, almost never characterized by acidity, but instead expressing an unexpected mineral freshness. These traits make it particularly suitable to accompany diverse dishes, from the rich Mediterranean cuisine to the spicy oriental one up to the most intense flavors of European cuisine: it just needs to be tried with a truffle-based first course to realize this.

TYPE: white, dry

COLOR: intense straw yellow, often tending to gold

BOUQUET: vigorous, with notes of rose petals, musk, elderflower, lychee, banana and citrus in general

TASTING NOTE: soft, pleasantly captivating and sustained by a light freshness

VARIETAL: Traminer Aromatico

DENOMINATION: Alto Adige DOC (Denomination of Controlled Origin)

REGION: Alto Adige, Italy

SERVING TEMPERATURE: 8/10°C

MINIMUM ALCOHOL CONTENT: 11%

PAIRING: oriental cuisine and courses from the sea – crustaceans starters, stuffed pastries and spicy meat in particular

VERDICCHIO
A GREAT ITALIAN WHITE

Within the fragmented enological landscape of Italian wines, a special mention goes to Verdicchio, produced from the namesake varietal in Marche, a region facing the Adriatic Sea. This is a particularly versatile varietal, capable of delivering excellent sparkling wines as well as charming passitos. However it can better express its elegant personality in the more traditional white vinification. Verdicchio is indeed a surprising wine, always multi-faceted and able to represent in detail the territory it comes from. Pleasantly floral and fruity, it stands out with notes of citrus and with a sure freshness, always supported by a certain structure. Moreover, Verdicchio has shown particular longevity compared to other Italian white wines, and so it can be appreciated even many years after the harvest.

What is considered as one of its elected areas, sits near the municipality of Jesi, in the province of Ancona, which looks out to the Appenines and Cupramontana from Senigallia. Cupramontana is particularly dedicated to the production of the best wines in the area. Here Verdicchio develops an extraordinary class and is structured with harmonious persistence. In the hinterland and around Matelica, on the other hand, it features fresher and more acidic traits, with an olfactory profile that goes from flowers to vegetation. Overall, wines of excellent purity. In both cases, Verdicchio can amaze in its easier and more immediate versions – so fragrant and pleasantly balanced – as well as in the more ambitious versions, often put on the market after 2 years from the harvest. The result is a deep and articulated wine. The outstanding wine is today carefully produced by an ever increasing number of wineries; those same wineries that in a couple of decades have managed to show all the excellence of this Italian white wine.

TYPE: white, dry

COLOR: straw-yellow

BOUQUET: fine and pleasantly intense, with notes of acacia and hawthorn, peach, apple, citrus and vaguely vegetable

TASTING NOTE: fresh, elegant, with a good balance between sapidity and acidity

VARIETAL: Verdicchio

DENOMINATION: Castelli di Jesi Verdicchio Riserva DOCG (Denomination of Controlled and Guaranteed Origin), Verdicchio di Matelica Riserva DOCG, Verdicchio dei Castelli di Jesi DOC (Denomination of Controlled Origin), Verdicchio di Matelica DOC

REGION: Marche, Italy

SERVING TEMPERATURE: 8/10°C

MINIMUM ALCOHOL CONTENT: 10.50%

PAIRING: main courses from the sea – soups, salads and seasoned focaccia in particular

VOUVRAY
THE CHARM OF THE LOIRE VALLEY

As one of the most famous French wine making regions, the Loire Valley stretches for a few hundred km from east to west in the northernmost part of the country. It offers an enchanting landscape, which every year attracts a large number of tourists eager to venture into its villages and distinctive castles.

Although being renowned mostly for its white wines, the area can offer a truly outstanding variety: extremely pure reds, charming sparkling wines and sweet wines full of personality. All of them have a common denominator: fresh acidity. This has mostly to do with the regional climate, which is rather temperate despite the latitude, with mild summers and fresh winters. Within this context the Cabernet Franc, Sauvignon Blanc and Chenin Blanc varietals find the right conditions to express grace and elegance along with Melon de Bourgogne, a varietal similar to Chardonnay which is used to make the famous Muscadet from Nantes. Chenin Blanc in particular truly represents the area: despite becoming quite popular in other countries such as South Africa and the United States, only in the area of Vouvray, east of the town of Tours, it can expose its enchanting character.

The best Vouvray wines are in fact capable of a surprising intensity and grace, with noble notes of ripened apple, walnuts, oriental spices and honey. Their complexity always anticipates a fresh taste; in their best versions, a sip is always accompanied by vehement acidity and great persistence. Moreover, although unusual for a not particularly warm and structured wine, the great Vouvray is capable of incredible longevity, even decades-long.

Despite the most popular version being the dry one – *sec* in French – the product specification contemplates various types: there are excellent examples of Vouvray "abboccati" – the so-called *sec-tendre* wines – and the *demi-sec, moelleux* and *doux* varieties are sweeter wines. Following these, are the increasingly popular *pétillant* – sparkling versions. The choice of what type to produce is mainly influenced by how the season develops; if the harvest is the result of an essentially warm year, the wine maker is therefore prone to produce more sugary wines. On the other hand, if the harvest is cooler, then the production veers towards drier wines. This is a general guideline which becomes really useful when trying to understand the labels of Vouvray, which remains one of the most unexpectedly surprising and captivating wines of the whole France.

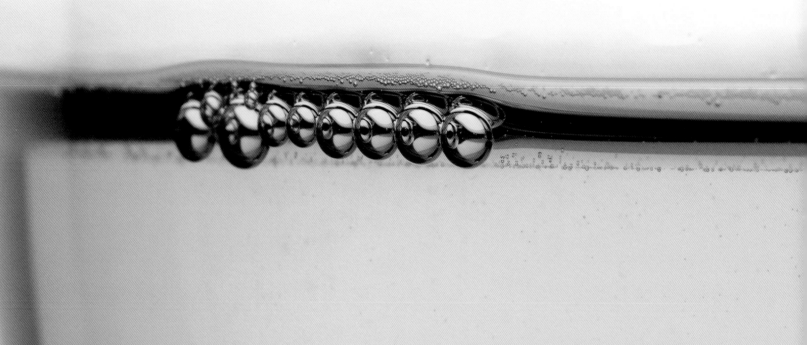

TYPE: white, dry
COLOR: straw-yellow
BOUQUET: ample and captivating with notes of lemon,
citrus and candied fruit, apple, pear, acacia and honey
TASTING NOTE: dry, elegant, with a sharp acidity
and great persistence
VARIETAL: Chenin Blanc
DENOMINATION: Vouvray AOC (Appellation
of controlled Origin)
REGION: Loire Valley, France
SERVING TEMPERATURE: 8/10°C
MINIMUM ALCOHOL CONTENT: 11%
PAIRING: vegetarian cuisine and main courses from
the sea – salads, oven-baked and grilled fish in particular

THE ENTHRALLING CHARM
OF RED WINES

It is no coincidence that some of the most famous and celebrated wines in the world are red; they often represent the best that wine makers can create in a certain location by working on the varietals that have managed to adapt to the characteristics – climatic and non – of that particular geographical area. It is possible to produce excellent Pinot Noirs in many parts of the world; but they will never acquire the unique characteristics of the best Gevrey-Chambertin wines produced in France. The same can be said for the Sangiovese and Brunello wines in Montalcino, Italy, or for Tempranillo and Rioja in Spain. And so on and so forth.

What is surprising about red wines is the impressive fragrance range that they possess, with scents that can beautifully transcend the more immediately recognizable traits of red fruits, which are typical of almost all red wines. Cherry, strawberry, plum, black cherry, blueberry, raspberry, blackberries and currants are the olfactory elements that describe the first, more immediate aspect of the wines. It is however during the fusion and evolution of these components that the magic of the wine's fragrance happens. Sometimes those essences blend with the scents given off by the wood in which the wines are aged, allowing time to generate gorgeously pure and intense bouquets. The best red wines are able to combine all these notes into a true symphony, as a demonstration of how the final result is superior to the simple sum of all the components. Along with such richness comes a unique gustatory texture; the best red wines perfectly represent the fusion of freshness and structure within an elegant context, where the quality of the taste is the protagonist.

Red wines come from the most disparate locations, challenging the geography of latitude and heights. France is for instance the birthplace of some of the most celebrated red wines in the world; the area of Bordeaux, Burgundy and the Rhine Valley facing the Mediterranean Sea. Italy stands out as well, thanks especially to Tuscany, Piedmont and the incredible Campania, which is abundant with some extremely impressive offers. Not to mention Spain. Furthermore, the international landscape is flourishing now more than ever, with incredibly intriguing wines; from Chile to California, not to mention South Africa with its red wines rich with personality. Discovering each one of them has never been so exciting.

AMARONE DELLA VALPOLICELLA
SOFTNESS AND ELEGANCE

Fruity, rich, soft, extraordinarily intense: as the most famous of the wines produced in the vast area of Verona in Veneto, Amarone della Valpolicella can give such a warm, welcoming sensation, like only a few other Italian wines manage to do. Produced in the hills overlooking the town of Romeo and Juliet, in just a few decades it has been able to stand out in the international scene in an ever growing crescendo of success. A fairly recent scenario, Amarone is an evolution of Recioto della Valpolicella, the traditional passito from the same area. Due to its fermentation naturally stopping at the first signs of winter, the latter was characterized by an unmistakable sugar residue. However, as time passed and seasons changed, its dry variation was initially born as a "mistake": the story goes that the first Amarone wines were those left behind in the barrels, perhaps in a corner of the cellar, and therefore left to complete their alcoholic fermentation, allowing the sweet component in the must to disappear. Thanks to these unique features, this bitter (as the name "Amarone" suggests) yet structured red wine has been able to find its own market in a very short time. It happened at the dawn of the 20th century: what some producers thought to be a mistake, would become one of the most iconic wines of the peninsula in less than a century.

The uniqueness of Amarone della Valpolicella is not due only to its birth, it is indeed a result of its production process: as an extreme rarity in the landscape of international wines, it is a dry wine coming from dried grapes. Along with other varietals, Corvina – the prominent and most well-known grape varietal used in its production – is traditionally harvested between the end of September and the beginning of October. Only the best grapes, the healthiest and ripest are selected for the production of Amarone; the grapes are placed to dry on straw mats inside vast and perfectly ventilated chambers. That's when the crucial phase starts: three/four months during which the grapes dry and lose up to 30% of their weight without succumbing to the mold that would inevitably compromise the quality of the wine. Between January and February the vinification process starts with the grapes being crushed: the best producers don't revert to any tool that can artificially increase the temperature, but they instead wait for nature to follow its course. A several weeks-long fermentation on the skins and a slow aging in wood – ranging from large oak barrels to the more modern Barriques – develop wines which are surprisingly nuanced in their articulation and depth. In other words, wines of great substance.

Moreover, the producers in the area have with time learned how to exploit the residues from the production of Amarone to give more roundness to their simpler, more immediate wine: Valpolicella. Instead of being thrown away, the pomace is mixed with the last harvest of wine for 2-3 weeks, during which it releases a small part of its extracts, therefore slightly altering the structure. That is how the famous Ripasso is produced: a red wine that, although only in a minor way, takes advantage of the drying process typical of this area near Verona.

Amarone della Valpolicella is unique: a consistently intense red wine, extraordinarily complex, as much fruity as pleasurably spicy, deep and enthralling. Standing out for its softness, despite the lack of intervention of the tannins, it is a wine that nevertheless expresses its elegance and grace over time. In its best interpretations, it can hugely surprise even long after harvesting. A wine that can delight you.

TYPE: red, dry
COLOR: dark ruby red, intense and impenetrable
BOUQUET: intense and complex with spicy notes of cherry, black cherry, tobacco, chocolate and licorice and dried fruits
TASTING NOTE: soft, full, warm and vigorous, with great persistence
VARIETAL: Corvina, Corvinone, Rondinella
DENOMINATION: Amarone della Valpolicella DOC (Denomination of Controlled Origin)
REGION: Veneto, Italy
SERVING TEMPERATURE: 16/18°C
MINIMUM ALCOHOL CONTENT: 14%
PAIRING: main courses from the land – risotto and roasted meat in particular

BARBARESCO
A MARVEL IN THE LANGHE

Although Barolo is the most distinguished wine not only in Piedmont but in Italy overall, the entire area of Langhe is extraordinarily consecrated to the cultivation of Nebbiolo: a red varietal which is common in other areas of the region but it is only in the vast tongue of land between the provinces of Cuneo and Asti that it manages to give supremely deep and incomparably elegant wines.

The wines coming from the small municipality of Barbaresco, a few km northwest of Alba, have for decades been considered substitutes of the more prestigious red Barolo. Only in the 1970s and 1980s, thanks to ever-increasing production and to the entrepreneurship of a few wine makers, that the wines of Neive, Treiso and in general the whole denomination, have started to attract the interest they deserve. As a land forever dedicated to the cultivation of grapes, the first official reference to a Barbaresco wine dates back to 1799: inside a document of the local parish is the story of an official of the Austrian Army who, after the victory over the French, ordered "...that a *carrà* (local truck-born barrel) of excellent Nebbiolo be brought to the base camp of Bra". In the 19th century the wine would mainly play a small role within the broader agricultural context; rarely bottled, it was mostly destined exclusively for household consumption.

Everything changed in 1894 when Domizio Cavazza, director of the Royal School of Enology in Alba, purchased the Castle of Barbaresco and founded what became the first cooperative in the area. It was a presence of extreme vivacity for that time: within its compound they would codify the production methodology which is still used today. Moreover, the cooperative would go the extra mile to promote Barbaresco outside the regional boundaries. Unfortunately it was just a flash in the pan, as it closed in 1922. In 1958, thanks to the vital input of the parish priest, a new body emerged with the intent of protecting the farmers from the ups and downs of the grape market, but also focusing on continuing the work started by Cavazza, universally considered the father of Barbaresco.

For many decades the timbre of Barbaresco and Barolo was, and still is, down to a relatively late harvest, an extremely slow maceration on skins and a long fermentation in big oak barrels. Despite all similarities, Barbaresco can historically boast some subtle differences compared to Barolo: an often softer tannic texture, a more welcoming fruity profile and a better readability when young. These features show not only the uniqueness of Barbaresco but also the excellent variety of red wines from the region of Langhe: they are indeed always amongst the best wines in Italy.

TYPE: red, dry
COLOR: light garnet red
BOUQUET: intense, with notes of red fruits (even as jam), violet, nutmeg, roasted hazelnut, tobacco and cocoa
TASTING NOTE: dry, pleasantly tannic, full and harmonic
VARIETAL: Nebbiolo
DENOMINATION: Barbaresco DOCG (Denomination of Controlled and Guaranteed Origin)
REGION: Piedmont, Italy
SERVING TEMPERATURE: 16/18°C
MINIMUM ALCOHOL CONTENT: 12%
PAIRING: main courses from the land – game, braised meat and aged cheese in particular

BAROLO
THE KING OF ITALIAN WINES

Endowed with an elegant yet strong and deep touch, Barolo – the red wine symbol of the Langhe region in south Piedmont, Italy – boasts a longevity that only a few other Italian and international wines possess. Thanks to its natural distinctive acidity and a pronounced phenolic content, Barolo is delightful in its youth; although with aging it exudes magnificence and grace, typical of the best red wines worldwide.

Moreover, the peculiarities of the territory where it is produced lead Barolo to present itself with unique diversity; moving from one vineyard to another, sometimes just a few hundred meters apart, one can see just how important the territory of cultivation is for the definition of a wine in all its versions. This diversity refers to different types of soil, sun exposition, heights and, last but not least, different production styles. It is no coincidence that some of the most relevant "additional geographical references" – as some of the local Crus are defined – have different owners who produce wines that subsequently can be slightly different from one another. From Cannubi to Bussia, from Monvigliero to Bricco Boschis up to Vigna Rionda, the whole denomination is dotted with what are regarded as legendary plots of land. The common grounds as well as the divergences that such diversity sparks, make the journey to discovering Barolo one of the most fascinating of the whole peninsula.

Obviously this hasn't always been the case; despite grape cultivation being a long tradition of the Langhe region, the history of Barolo is relatively recent. Around the middle of the 19th century, they started to produce a "French-like" red wine thanks to the input of Juliette Cobert – also known as Marchioness Giulia Falletti di Barolo – and Count Camill Benso di Cavour. Only a few years later, that wine signified the Italian unification by being the protagonist on the tables of the then most illustrious city in Italy: Turin. In a brief period of time, the territory attracted ever growing attention by laying the foundations of the first estates and their production equipment. The production system had already been codified: a long resting period in big oak barrels was necessary for the wine to dry completely, removing all sugar residues and smoothing its natural young sharpness at the same time.

Nowadays the production area – the municipalities of Barolo, Castiglione Falletto, Serralunga d'Alba and partly Monforte d'Alba, Novello, La Morra, Verduno, Grinzane Cavour, Diano d'Alba, Cherasco and Roddi, all in the province of Cuneo – offers an incredibly rich production heterogeneity, with many of the entities involved offering disparate approaches.

TYPE: *red, dry*
COLOR: *light garnet red*
BOUQUET: *ample, pleasantly ethereal with notes
of withered roses and violets, raspberries,
wild strawberries, dried mushrooms, white truffle,
wet earth, tobacco, leather and menthol*
TASTING NOTE: *dry, pleasantly tannic and very pure*
VARIETAL: *Nebbiolo*
DENOMINATION: *Barolo DOCG (Denomination
of Controlled and Guaranteed Origin)*
REGION: *Piedmont, Italy*
SERVING TEMPERATURE: *16/18°C*
MINIMUM ALCOHOL CONTENT: *12.5%*
PAIRING: *main courses from the land – game,
braised meat and aged cheese in particular*

One of the most debatable techniques, at least up to a few years ago, regards the type of barrel to use for the best aging of Barolo. Traditionalists used to identify the past as the only key to interpret their wine; modernists, on the other hand, identified the small French barrel – the Barrique – as an essential tool if wanting to produce the best wine possible. Nowadays the different approaches to vinification, as well as to the practices that lead to the birth of Barolo, coexist under the same roof and are less emphasized than before. This is proof of the talent of Nebbiolo, a varietal that can adapt to nature as well as to craftsmanship; in the area of Barolo, it delivers extraordinary wines, with an olfactory profile ranging from flowers to fruits. After a few years aging in the bottle, it shifts to extremely pleasant tertiary scents that recall leather, mushrooms and truffle. However these are only a few of the recognizable traits of this unmistakably charming, fresh, powerful and fulfilling wine: worth waiting for and worth discovering.

One of the prominent characteristics of Nebbiolo grapes is linked to their ripening; historically Nebbiolo is the last varietal to be harvested in the Langhe region, between the end of October and the beginning of November.

BRUNELLO DI MONTALCINO
THE CHARM OF THE NOBLEST TUSCAN WINE

Although the phenomenon of Brunello di Montalcino as an internationally acclaimed wine is relatively recent, it cannot be denied that the vocation of that territory for producing excellent wine has been known for centuries. In his "Description of Italy",1550, Leandro Alberti, a friar from Bologna, mentioned Montalcino as a distinguished town "for its good wine that comes from those pleasant hills". It was no coincidence. During the Middle Ages, Montalcino was fortunate enough to sit on that route still known today as the Via Francigena, one of the roads that connected the north of Italy and the north of Europe to Rome. Through the centuries, travelers of all kinds stopped by in its lodging houses and ate in its taverns, creating traffic that fed into a constant and copious wine production. At that time, the most common was Moscadello, a slightly sweet white. However, with the gradual change in tastes all over Europe, it wasn't long before a dry red was born: the father of the current Brunello was a long barrel-aged wine produced solely from grapes of the local Sangiovese varietal.

It was mainly during the 1800's that Brunello acquired the form it still retains today. One of the most ancient pieces of evidence concerning a red wine of Montalcino dates back to 1875 and is by the Ampelographic Commission of the Province of Siena: a Brunello of 1843 which was described as a ruby red wine, with a level of alcohol, acidity and extracts that could easily be compared to the best contemporary wines. The following century saw export flourishing, although the whole production system in the area was hit very hard by the threat of the Phylloxera epidemic, the two World Wars and the end of sharecropping. It was only from the 1970's and thanks to huge private investments that the world started talking about Montalcino and its wines again.

The Montalcino area, south-east of the town of Siena, benefits from a rather stable and mild Mediterranean climate, with a great deal of clear days throughout the whole vegetative phase of the life of the grapes, between spring and summer.

The area also benefits from the shelter given by Mount Amiata, which acts as a natural shield against particularly intense calamities, such as floods and hail-storms. It is an ideal site not only for the cultivation of grapes but also for the full ripening of the Sangiovese, by far the most important varietal throughout the whole of Tuscany.

The key characteristic of Brunello di Montalcino is directly related to its long and slow aging in the winery, which results in at least 5 years having to pass between the harvest and the wine hitting the market. During this period the wine is left to age in differently sized barrels – from the traditional bigger ones to the modern Barrique – and so it acquires its unique features. Its harmony and elegance, impossible to replicate anywhere else, make Brunello special the moment it is put on the market, as well as after decades from the harvest. It is one of the most reliable and long-lived Italian red wines.

TYPE: red, dry
COLOR: ruby red often tending to garnet
BOUQUET: ample, with notes of small red fruit (even in jam), mixed berries, withered flowers, mushrooms, black truffle and cinnamon
TASTING NOTE: elegant, harmonious, dry, with good acidity and great persistence
VARIETAL: Sangiovese
DENOMINATION: Brunello di Montalcino DOCG (Denomination of Controlled and Guaranteed Origin)
REGION: Tuscany, Italy
SERVING TEMPERATURE: 16/18°C
MINIMUM ALCOHOL CONTENT: 12.5%
PAIRING: main courses from the land, mushroom-based dishes, grilled meat and roasted game

CHÂTEAUNEUF-DU-PAPE
MORE THAN JUST THE WINE OF THE POPES

The village of Châteauneuf-du-Pape, although small in size, produces a wine of huge impact from its surrounding hills. As a red of extraordinary charm, it has always been considered one of the best ambassadors of wine-making France for its depth and longevity. It is a wine of great territorial affinity: being interpreted in many different ways but still always intriguing, it is so neatly defined by a certain structure and a Mediterranean style generosity.

It is no coincidence that its denomination includes as many as 13 different varietals. The most common are Grenache, Mourvedre and Syrah, all of them present in different proportions in almost every wine of the area. Following these are small percentages of Cinsaut, Muscardin, Counoise and others, to name just the most well-known. The first one though – Grenache, is the one that characterizes each wine from the area: a wine varietal that creates warm, soft and rounded wines, with low acidity, intense olfactory sensations and, last but not least, enough body to please the palate even after many years.

Châteauneuf-du-Pape wines are produced in a small area at the heart of one of the more prominent wine making areas in France: the enchanting southern Rhone Valley, so alluring for its landscapes and climate. The area stretches mostly to the north of the town of Avignon, not far from Provence and the Mediterranean Sea. Here in 1309 Pope Clement V relocated the papal court, opening that historical period called the "Avignon papacy". Over a period of 68 years, the entire papacy was transferred from Italy to France: it was widespread opinion that the city of Rome, which was caught in internal fights between the most powerful families, was not safe enough for the Pope. The presence of the papal court in Avignon and of the whole economy attached to it, provoked the fast development of grape cultivation in the entire area, creating the foundations of the wines we know today.

Apart from red wines, the area produces a small yet significant amount of white wines. The soft and fruity Grenache Blanc and Roussanne varietals work side by side with Bourboulenc, Clairette and Picpoul, which complement with their more subtle, mineral and floral aromatic profile. Entering the constantly evolving display of the red wines, Châteauneuf-du-Pape has become one of the most interesting denominations of the country.

TYPE: red, dry

COLOR: intense ruby red

BOUQUET: deep with notes of wild strawberry, cherries, berries, wet earth, black pepper and vanilla

TASTING NOTE: warm, soft, harmonic and pleasantly persistent

VARIETAL: Grenache, Mourvedre and Syrah

DENOMINATION: Châteauneuf-du-Pape AOC (Appellation of Controlled Origin)

REGION: Rhone, France

SERVING TEMPERATURE: 16/18°C

MINIMUM ALCOHOL CONTENT: 12.5%

PAIRING: main courses from the land – game, roasts and aged cheese in particular

CHIANTI CLASSICO
TUSCANY IN ITS HEART

In the vast area that separates the Tuscan cities of Florence and Siena, one of the most prestigious Italian wines is produced: Chianti Classico. The unmistakable Sangiovese-based red wine can surprise in its youth with a peculiar fragrance, as well as acquiring an increasing depth with aging. With the passing of time, certain notes of violet and maraschino cherry beautifully blend with smoky scents of tar, cigar tobacco and cocoa. What remains immutable is the ability of Chianti Classico to hold on to a certain freshness even after many years, which allows it to unfold into a particularly noble version.

This is no coincidence: the whole area where it is produced is rich with history closely linked to the production of wine. The hills of Chianti Classico have been hosting the cultivation of grapes for more than 2000 years, as a tradition dating back to the Romans and Etruscans. However what is considered as the most important historical period for the local wine started at the end of the Middle Ages, when the local vineyards began to spread across the area, creating that rich productive fabric that still characterizes the Chianti Classico region. The first document where a wine is defined as Chianti dates back to the end of the 14th century, and just 200 years later there is evidence of batches of local wine being shipped abroad, to the table of the English Court in particular. In 1716 the Grand Duke of Tuscany Cosimo III, issued an edict to protect its name and clearly define its borders. It was the first time in Europe that a production area was delineated in such detail. The denomination still exists today. The Chianti Classico area stretches for over 70,000 hectares in the following municipalities: Castellina in Chianti, Gaiole in Chianti, Greve in Chianti, Radda in Chianti and partly Barberino Val d'Elsa, Castelnuovo Berardenga, Poggibonsi, San Casciano in Val di Pesa and Tavarnelle Val di Pesa. This is the historical region, which is not to be confused with that of the more common Chianti wine, a red wine produced in most parts of Tuscany and considered less prestigious than Chianti Classico.

The predominant Sangiovese varietal – which must be at least 80% of the content, as specified in the current product specification – is complemented by the typical minor Tuscan varietals of Canaiolo and Colorino, and sometimes by the more international Merlot and Cabernet Sauvignon. This has not always been the case though. Already in 1872 some wineries would distinguish 2 wines: one more ambitious and suitable for aging and another one, more immediate and suitable for everyday consumption. The latter would include a small percentage of Malvasia, a white grape varietal that would accentuate aromas and freshness.

TYPE: red, dry

COLOR: ruby red

BOUQUET: complex, with notes of blackberries and raspberries, iris, sweet violet and vanilla and cinnamon

TASTING NOTE: dry, harmonic, with good acidity and great persistence

VARIETAL: Sangiovese

DENOMINATION: Chianti Classico DOCG (Denomination of Controlled and Guaranteed Origin)

REGION: Tuscany, Italy

SERVING TEMPERATURE: 16/18°C

MINIMUM ALCOHOL CONTENT: 12%

PAIRING: main courses from the land – char-grilled meat in particular

Over time the Trebbiano varietal was introduced as well; such a practice made many Chianti Classico wines become too simple, compared to the history and the blazon they had acquired up to that point. That is why in around the 1970s many wine makers decided to bottle their best red wines without the name Chianti Classico but as simple "table wines", as a sign of protest against the excessive fragmentation that the denomination had reached. This way the "Super Tuscans", as an important American magazine defined them years later, were born: these gorgeous wines can conjugate the best territorial characteristics with the best features of their varietals – particularly the most popular ones, Sangiovese and Cabernet Sauvignon. For this reason, since 2006 it is no longer possible to use white grape varietals for the production of the local red wines.

What is certain is that the entire region is currently living in an extraordinarily exciting productive moment: the differences are to be found more in the geological and climatic diversity of the single municipalities and in the different stylistic approaches of the wineries, rather than in the use of the Barrique or the big barrel – just to mention one of the most debated choices of recent years. In such a productive landscape, each glass tastes different: more or less pure, more or less structured and acidic, diverse tannic nuances, etc. are just a few of the peculiar traits of a wine that maintains an overall purity, articulation and complexity, whether just bottled or after years of aging. These are all good reasons that make Chianti Classico one of the most exciting red wines in Italy.

Chianti Classico boasts different geological characteristics; in the northernmost area of the denomination for instance, the soils rich in clay deliver robust and intense wines

GEVREY-CHAMBERTIN
THE PURITY OF THE CÔTE DE NUITS

There is no other place in the world whose vineyards are as famous as those surrounding the small municipality of Gevrey-Chambertin, in the heart of the Côte de Nuits, in the northernmost part of Burgundy and the Côte d'Or. 26 vineyards are listed as Premier Cru and 9 as Grand Cru; the latter are all situated immediately south of the town center, along the hill crest that stretches towards the municipal borders of Morey-St-Denis. Chambertin, Chambertin-Clos de Bèze, Charmes-Chambertin, Mazoyères-Chambertin, Chapelle-Chambertin, Griotte-Chambertin, Latricières-Chambertin, Mazis-Chambertin and Ruchottes-Chambertin are some of the finest quality red wines in the whole world. This is where wines of incomparable grace, purity, detail, richness and longevity are produced. They represent the quintessential Pinot Noir; its olfactory profile ignites sparks of pleasure, thanks to unmistakable notes of small red fruits that in the first years combine with scents of mulberry, violet and rose. Later on in the years, it evolves into noble notes of licorice and leather with hints of undergrowth. Upon tasting, these wines also impress for their structure and velvety tannic texture. Bodied, powerful, rich yet at the same time elegant, they are able to delight even after decades, possibly unlike any other wine in the rest of the world.

Within this exceptional area of Burgundy the specific soil characteristics work along with a perfect geographical exposure and a favorable position that shield the vineyards from the northern winds. It is therefore no coincidence that recent archaeological excavations have revealed that Burgundy wine was born in Gevrey-Chambertin, where the first vines were planted over 2000 years ago. Like most part of the viticulture regulations in Burgundy, the denomination was created in 1936 – an extremely important year for the official designation of Premier and Grand Cru as well. Some Premier Cru wines stand out for their fame: Lavaut Saint-Jacques, Les Cazetiers, Clos des Varoilles and above all Clos Saint-Jacques, one of the most popular Premier Cru wines in the entire region, which many have considered at the same level as the best Grand Crus. Furthermore, as a rather isolated case in Burgundy, the vineyards that can be named on the label as being part of the Village of Gevrey-Chambertin, also extend east of the road that crosses the valley, thus demonstrating the extraordinary vocation of the entire area that surrounds the town center.

TYPE: red, dry
COLOR: ruby red
BOUQUET: ample, pure, with notes of wild strawberries,
raspberries, mulberry, black currant, blackberries,
blueberries, earth, vanilla, pink pepper and licorice
TASTING NOTE: elegant, powerful, reactive and with
a great persistence
VARIETAL: Pinot Noir
DENOMINATION: Gevrey-Chambertin AOC
(Appellation of Controlled Origin)
REGION: Burgundy, France
SERVING TEMPERATURE: 16/18°C
MINIMUM ALCOHOL CONTENT: 10.5%
PAIRING: main courses from the land –
roasts and aged cheese in particular

HERMITAGE
IN THE HEART OF THE RHONE VALLEY

Wines produced with Syrah – one of the most glorious French varietals – are commonly known for their spicy olfactory profile; easily linked to a charming and enthralling black pepper note, Syrah delivers wines with good structure and excellent balance. It is therefore no coincidence that this varietal has over time found fertile ground almost everywhere in the world – California, Chile, South Africa, Australia, etc.

However it is in the Rhone Valley, in South-Eastern France, that the Syrah grape comes into its own. In the heart of the region, not far north of the town of Valence, it is possible to find a small denomination that has always offered some of the most celebrated, elegant and long-lived wines of the country: Hermitage. In his book "Topographie de tous les vignobles connus" (The Topography of all the Known Vineyards), published in1816, the enologist and writer André Jullien included this 140 hectares-vast plot of land amongst the best in the world, on the same level as Bordeaux and Burgundy. It is such an individual place: packed with vineyards, it conveniently faces south along the hillside, where the Rhone, the largest French river, runs by.

With gripping intensity, a young Hermitage wine features an extraordinary fruity profile, along with a powerful tannic texture and a strong structure. After a few years its impetuosity gradually fades into an unrivaled elegance and vastness, without losing that vigor which represents its most natural timbre. It is a charming red: the noble evolution of its olfactory traits – a certain balsamic and intriguing spiciness – always seems to serve something higher and more complex. They never evolve just for their own sake. This is what makes Hermitage unique in the landscape of Syrah-based wines. This is what makes the northern Rhone Valley special and famous for the cultivation of grapes and the production of the wines. From Crozes-Hermitage to St-Joseph, the entire area is renowned for red wines produced from Syrah grapes. It is simply not possible to remain indifferent to them.

An interesting note: the area of Hermitage is also known for the production of an excellent white, based on the Marsanne and Roussanne varietals, which occupy roughly a quarter of the whole denomination. It is a rarely captivating wine, in no way inferior to the namesake red for its aromatic intensity and longevity.

TYPE: red, dry
COLOR: dark ruby red
BOUQUET: intense, with notes of wild blackberries, cherry, blueberries, black pepper, wet earth, chocolate and cocoa
TASTING NOTE: intense, tannic, powerful, with a vibrant persistence
VARIETAL: Syrah
DENOMINATION: Hermitage AOC (Appellation of Controlled Origin)
REGION: Rhone, France
SERVING TEMPERATURE: 16/18°C
MINIMUM ALCOHOL CONTENT: 10.5%
PAIRING: main courses from the land – game, roasted and stewed meat in particular

Although the Syrah varietal expresses its full potential in the Rhone valley, excellent versions can be found in the United States and Australia.

145

MONTEFALCO SAGRANTINO
POWER AND AUSTERITY

The best time to visit Montefalco and its surrounding districts is between the end of October and the beginning of November. That's when the vineyards of Sagrantino, the most typical and prestigious wine varietal of the area, take on that uniquely intense red shade that covers the hills like a beautiful blanket.

However, things have not always been like they are now: the dry version of Montefalco Sagrantino was born only in the seventies and has become commercially successful only since the late nineties onwards. In such a fermenting time frame, the vineyards have multiplied in all 5 districts that belong to this denomination, from Bevagna up to Gualdo Cattaneo, Giano and Castel Ritaldi. Such a sudden prosperity is far from the slow pace that this particular area of Umbria had followed for centuries, with its bond with tradition passing from one generation to the next. It is not a coincidence that the name itself "Sagrantino" most probably derives from the term "sacrament" (from the Latin *sacer*, sacred). It is indeed to the monks inhabiting the area that stretches from Assisi towards Montefalco and Spoleto, that the Sagrantino's conservation process owes its existence: the sweet wine is the result of patient withering of the best grapes on the traditional branches for a few weeks, then used in religious rituals as well as during the most important occasions, when peasants would open a bottle to share with their families.

Although it almost disappeared during the last century, the wine has bravely regained its deserved place and current popularity with an innovative dry version, thanks to a few local wineries. The powerful red wine stands out for its structure and longevity, both being the result of the extraordinary abundance of polyphenols and tannins in its grapes. The wine therefore needs long cellar maturation and refining in a bottle, in order to soften its natural austerity and to bring back that beautiful fusion, typical of its best interpretations. The secret is keeping a few bottles aside and going back to them periodically over the years; it won't fail to surprise you.

TYPE: red, dry

COLOR: dark red, intense and impenetrable

BOUQUET: complex and deep with notes of bramble, plums (even as jam), cherry, violet, vanilla, licorice

TASTING NOTE: full, rich, intense and sharp tannic texture, great persistence

VARIETAL: Sagrantino

DENOMINATION: Montefalco Sagrantino DOCG (Denomination of Controlled and Guaranteed Origin)

REGION: Umbria, Italy

SERVING TEMPERATURE: 16/18°C

MINIMUM ALCOHOL CONTENT: 13.5%

PAIRING: main courses from the land – stewed and braised meat in particular

PAÍS
CHILEAN PRIDE

The first settlers coming mainly from Spain and Portugal systematically planted the first vineyards in South America; however, a long time had to pass – indicatively up to the end of the last century – to see a widespread growth of quality wines produced in that continent. Argentina, Chile and, in a minor way, Brazil, are countries that today can boast a production vivacity capable of attracting a lot of interest towards them. This upheaval has roots not only in the increasing experience of its protagonists but also in a new way to look at its own unique features with pride without trying to replicate other models, especially European ones.

Chile in particular is perhaps the country which during the last fifty years has managed to grow in terms of quantity and variety of wines produced. It is an extraordinarily heterogeneous country for its climate and its lands; new regions have stood out in a little time, generating wines very different from each other. It is no coincidence that in the last few years new labels have been introduced, with terms like Costa, Entre Cordilleras and Andes to specify the different production areas, from the ones closer to the ocean to those in the hinterland, towards the mountain chain of the Andes. The French wine varietals have always been the ones to be in the spotlight when it comes to extraordinary variety: from Cabernet Sauvignon, the most famous and widespread varietal in Chile, up to Chardonnay and Sauvignon Blanc.

In recent times, there has been increasing interest in País, a wine produced from the namesake varietal, which is a close relative to Criolla Chica in Argentina and Mission in Mexico and the United States. Most probably brought to Chile as a seed by the Spanish conquistadors, the varietal has quickly adapted to the dry climate of the south. As an extremely rare case, whilst Europe's vineyards were literally swept away in the 1800's by Phylloxera, the parasite never arrived in the country, thanks to its geographical isolation. This uniqueness has ever since allowed Chile to benefit from plots of land with ungrafted vines, i.e. grown on their own roots, that are over 200 years old, unlike the rest of the vineyards in the world that adopted the technique of grafting the European vine on to an American rootstock in order to combat the devastating disease. Many of these stunning vineyards, often grown with the lovely shape of small trees, are País, another reason for wine makers to look at this ancient varietal with a lot of attention.

Although for a long time País wines were very simple, fresh and fruity, sold unpackaged and destined for immediate use, they have recently started to attract a great deal of interest. An emerging idea has started to make its own way in Chile: that a possible new future really could be in the hands of País, as a wine capable of a newly discovered fragrance and gustatory depth.

TYPE: red, dry
COLOR: intense ruby red
BOUQUET: firm, with strong notes of cherry, currant, blueberry, withered rose, withered red flowers, wet earth, toasted oak
TASTING NOTE: balanced, fresh, pleasantly fragrant and with good structure
VARIETAL: País
DENOMINATION: Chilean wine
COUNTRY: Chile
SERVING TEMPERATURE: 16/18°C
MINIMUM ALCOHOL CONTENT: approximately 11/11.5%
PAIRING: main courses from the land – seasoned focaccia, meat tapas and pasta-based first courses in particular

PAUILLAC
BORDEAUX ESSENCE

The famous classification of Bordeaux wines in 1855, as the first of its genre, was created during the Universal Exhibition in Paris by request of Emperor Napoleon III. The intention was to offer people arriving in the capital a guideline that would help them understand the quality differences between the best French wines, at that time identified with Bordeaux. Therefore the classification had to take into consideration both the reputation of the numerous châteaux and the prices of their wines; the latter were at the time decided by those external mediators who would deal with buying and re-selling them.

Consequentially, only the red and sweet wines that were in greatest demand at the time were examined. The wines were classified in order of importance, from Premier Crus to Cinquième Crus. This quality pyramid has been modified only twice in 150 years: the first time in 1856 and the second over a century later, when a château – as a unique case – saw the passage from Deuxième Cru to Premier Cru officially recognized in 1973.

It is easy to imagine how much things have changed in such a long period of time; despite its fame and ambition to be the first one ever to be related to an agricultural product, the classification has been hit by harsh criticism. The main accusation relates to its immobility; it is possibly a very accurate snapshot of the situation of Médoc in the middle of the 1800s, but it is surely not representing the current situation anymore. Over time many other important entities were born and many of those original vineyards have seen their perimeter changing ownership, therefore affecting the accuracy of the classification made in 1855. What is sure is that the left bank of the Gironde is still regarded as the birthplace of some of the most famous wines ever. Also, it is no coincidence that Bordeaux hosts one of the most prestigious enological schools in the world; it gave input to the introduction of some popular wine making techniques and it continues to carry on flourishing research. For decades the best enologists in the world have come here to train, to then take the knowledge out to the other important viticultural areas worldwide.

In some areas of the Bordeaux region, the soils rich in silica contribute to the purity of the local wines.

Within the region the vastest and most famous area is that of Médoc: a territory subdivided into Bas-Médoc and Haut-Médoc, stretching from Bordeaux along the left bank of the Gironde and crossing some of the most important denominations. It is here that the Cabernet Sauvignon varietal is able to deliver elegant and undoubtedly classy wines, blessed with a unique expressiveness. Well-structured and long-lived, the red wines include a certain percentage of Cabernet Franc and Merlot too, that implements the structure as well as the roundness. These three varietals, sometimes along with Malbec and Petit Verdot, give the name to the famous and much replicated "Bordeaux blend".

If we could rank the most important *appellations* of Bordeaux, Pauillac would probably be the most quoted, as it is there that some of the most acclaimed French red wines are produced. Their organoleptic profile represents the essence of the region: structured and fresh, complex, fine and rich in details and long-lived. Their extensive vineyards surround the namesake town as far as the eye can see. The area is in fact known for the almost total absence of hills; the highest of them is no more than 30m high above sea level. These gorgeous wines are usually able to show their best after a long period of refining in the bottle, at least 10 years: a seemingly endless period of time, worth waiting for.

Cabernet Sauvignon is without doubt the most famous varietal in the world for the production of wines of great quality and longevity.

TYPE: red, dry

COLOR: intense ruby red, often tending to amber

BOUQUET: intense and rich, with hints of blackcurrant, blackberry, blueberry, cherry, tobacco, cigars, wet earth, cedar wood, graphite

TASTING NOTE: full, elegant and refined, pleasantly soft, with great persistence

VARIETAL: Cabernet Sauvignon

DENOMINATION: Pauillac AOC (Appellation of Controlled Origin)

REGION: Bordeaux, France

SERVING TEMPERATURE: 16/18°C

MINIMUM ALCOHOL CONTENT: 11%

PAIRING: main courses from the land – roasts and aged cheese in particular

PINOTAGE
A SOUTH AFRICAN STORY

The most notorious and widespread varietals – those we know and appreciate in their multiple forms – are usually the result of a centuries-long evolutionary process, during which the vineyards adapt to the climatic conditions of a certain place. On the other hand, it is not rare to come across laboratory-created varietals: those born from a cross between different types, in order to acquire the best characteristics of all the components.

This is the case of Pinotage, created in South Africa around the middle of the last century. In 1925 Abraham Izak Perold, Professor of Viticulture at the University of Stellenbosch, a small town east of Cape Town, thought of crossing the fine Pinot Noir – a varietal capable of delivering some of the best wines in the world – with the more robust Cinsault (at that time also called Hermitage), a varietal from the Rhone area with a safe structure and a certain warmth. The choice of these two varietals had some solid base: whereas the first could bring elegance and longevity, the second, which had adapted particularly well in the area, could contribute in terms of sugar and depth. However Perold didn't leave any written trace of his experiments at that time, and today we can only guess what ideas he had to back up his choices. Surely his knowledge of the subject was extremely vast; it was him, for instance, to lay the foundations for the experimental garden within the University, still active today. That garden could boast the most prestigious collection of wine varietals in the country, over 100. They were all varietals that Perold had collected during his trips to Europe.

From the crossing between Pinot Noir and Cinsault, only 4 seeds were produced; a ridiculously small quantity compared to the thousands of today. The fact that Perold decided to plant them in his own garden, instead of at the University, opens up to several speculations: it could have been to monitor their growth more closely or, at the same time, because he wasn't actually that sure about the result. Two years later, in 1927, after becoming the Principal of the Faculty of Viticulture, he left the University for private employment. It was only some time afterwards that a colleague of his remembered about those 4 seeds, just in time to bring them back to the University to study their developments.

The plants were multiplied and immediately their resistance stood out; this would make the varietal perfect for that area's climate. In 1943 the Pinotage varietal left the exclusively academic context to be used by a winery for commercial purpose.

Since then the South African wine has made great strides and today it is considered amongst the protagonists of that new world that has dominated the worldwide viticulture from the 1960s and 1970s onwards. Pinotage is currently produced by a small yet significant number of wineries and it is no coincidence that it is the most famous, despite the least relevant from a numerical point of view. It is a decisive, intense red, often characterized by notes of lacquer and paint, along with scents of blackberry, wild plum and mulberry, with a tannic texture anything but obvious and with a strong gustatory depth. A great ambassador of the country around the world.

TYPE: red, dry
COLOR: intense ruby red
BOUQUET: intense, with notes of prune, blackberry, raspberry, cherry, red pepper, paint, licorice, tobacco and tar
TASTING NOTE: full, deep, slightly tannic and with strong persistence
VARIETAL: Pinotage
DENOMINATION: South African wine
COUNTRY: South Africa
SERVING TEMPERATURE: 16/18°C
MINIMUM ALCOHOL CONTENT: Approximately 12/12.5%
PAIRING: courses from the land – soups, risotto and stews in particular

POMEROL
THE ENCLAVE OF MERLOT

Amongst the most popular varietals in the world, Merlot contributes to the success of many wines across the continents – from the United States to Australia and South Africa.

As a tiny area north-west of Saint-Émilion, Pomerol is universally recognized as the birthplace of one of the greatest Merlot-based red wines in the world. It is quite a rare case, because its denomination doesn't develop around a town area; it embraces a countryside that is quite homogeneous and flat, with a great number of vineyards and small local châteaux – a definition that includes widely different types of buildings.

The history of Pomerol is rather exclusive: the area of Bordeaux was renowned especially for Médoc and Graves wines, along with the sweet wines from around Sauternes and Barsac. It is only with the increasing fame of wines from the so called "right bank" of the Gironde – the river running across the Bordeaux influencing its climate in that unique way – that they slowly realized the immense quality of the wines produced in one of the easternmost areas of the region. As in many other wine-making locations in France and more generally in Europe, it is with the development of modern transport links that the wine has had the opportunity to become known outside of its boundaries, especially in the big cities. As an example, in 1853 the railway track that still today connects Libourne to Paris was completed. However it was only during the last century – the first product specification for Pomerol dates back to 1936 – and in particular the second half of the 1900s, that the area stepped up in quality, projecting itself amongst the most important and prestigious production areas of the world. It was a period of mounting excitement, both commercially and media wise, that saw attention towards Pomerol increasing as much as on other French red wines. Although possible to come across great red wines based on Merlot not only in the nearby Saint-Émilion or even in the American State of California, it is only in Pomerol that this particular varietal manages to deliver wines which are unique for their richness, complexity and elegance. Truly unforgettable wines.

From a geological point of view, the whole denomination sits on a vast pebbly sediment, which is sandier in the south and more clay-rich in the north, where wines acquire an extraordinary purity more than in any other area. The distinctive trait of Pomerol is its homogeneity, which wouldn't make for a very plausible classification to follow in the footsteps of Médoc's in 1855. That is not all: unlike in some other areas of Bordeaux, the majority of Pomerol wineries don't have a centuries-old history and except in rare cases, possess barely even a ten year-old one.

TYPE: red, dry

COLOR: intense ruby red often tending to garnet

BOUQUET: intense, with notes of black cherry, blackberry, yarrow, prune, withered violet, truffle, chocolate

TASTING NOTE: full, rich, elegant and harmonious

VARIETAL: Merlot, Cabernet Franc

DENOMINATION: Pomerol AOC (Appellation of Controlled Origin)

REGION: Bordeaux, France

SERVING TEMPERATURE: 16/18°C

MINIMUM ALCOHOL CONTENT: 11%

PAIRING: main courses from the land – roasts and aged cheese in particular

POMMARD
THE CHARACTER OF THE CÔTE DE BEAUNE

The history of Burgundy has been closely linked to its wines for about 2 thousand years, namely since the Romans brought over rooted vines, first for growing grapes and then for the production of household wine, in line with their customs. However it was only thanks to the local monks' painstaking work in the fields several centuries afterwards, that the foundations were laid for the wine that we know today. Monastic orders such as the Benedictines and Cistercians played a crucial role in carrying on taking care and protecting the vineyards through the generations; for the first time in history, they also selected the most wine-dedicated areas and identified them as Crus, i.e. special vineyards that would deliver uniquely characterized wines. Those plots of land, whose borders were defined by low stone walls, are still there today. In 1855 – the same year as the classification for the famous Bordeaux wines – the *Histoire et Statistique de la Vigne de Grands Vins de la Côte-d'Or* (*History and Statistics of the Vineyard of the Great Wines in the Côte-d'Or*) was published: for the first time it suggested to classify Burgundy wines in order of importance, therefore creating guidelines that still exist today.

The Côte d'Or, as the undisputed birthplace of the best Chardonnay and Pinot Noir-based wines worldwide, is conventionally divided into two equally highly valued subareas: the southern Côte de Beaune, which is the cradle of great white wines and the northern Côte de Nuits, which hosts the best red ones. It is in the area near the town of Beaune – considered to be the capital of Burgundy – that some of the most typical wines in the region are produced. It is a vast hilly strip of land entirely cultivated as Premier Cru, that stretches south up to the first houses of Pommard, a small town where some extremely intense and inebriating red wines are produced.

Impetuous in their youth as much as surprisingly long-lived, they set themselves apart from the more delicate wines produced further south in Volnay. Often characterized by a particularly marked tannic texture, they are unique in their ability to give off gorgeous scents of red berries with precious traits of cocoa, coffee and pink pepper that eventually develop into notes of tar. These characteristics can be traced in some of the most celebrated vineyards: those classified as Premier Cru are 27, although it goes without saying that wines such as Les Rugiens or Clos des Épeneaux are equally able to delight any enthusiast, having nothing to envy of the Grand Crus from the Côte de Nuits.

TYPE: red, dry
COLOR: ruby red
BOUQUET: intense, pure, with notes of black cherry, raspberry, rose, violet, aromatic herbs, cocoa, coffee, pink pepper and vanilla beans
TASTING NOTE: greatly balanced between freshness and tannic texture, harmonious, with excellent persistence
VARIETAL: Pinot Noir
DENOMINATION: Pommard AOC (Appellation of Controlled Origin)
REGION: Burgundy, France
SERVING TEMPERATURE: 16/18°C
MINIMUM ALCOHOL CONTENT: 10.5%
PAIRING: main courses from the land – game and aged cheese in particular

PRIORAT
CATALONIA'S MOST HIDDEN SECRET

As a small segment of land at the western end of Catalonia, not far from Tarragona, the area of Priorat is particularly hostile and rugged, difficult to cultivate due to its very steep hills. It has always been devoted to wine making; before the arrival of Phylloxera there were 5,000 hectares of land, shaping the landscape with their vineyards. Subsequent impoverishment of the entire region, additionally caused by Franco's strict policies, brought the majority of the population to abandon the countryside to venture for fortune in the nearby cities, especially Barcelona.

It is only since the 1980s that a few enlightened wine makers have started to believe again in the unique potential of this area, the secret of which is represented by its geological features. On one side it is protected from the northern winds by the spectacular mountain chain of Serra de Montsant; on the other side, the whole Priorat territory is characterized by *llicorella*, a specific brown slate rich in quartz, which contributes strongly to the personality of the wines.

The red wines produced from the traditional varietals of Garnacha and Cariñena stand out for their freshness, depth and substance. Wines of great, superb elegance. These traits have allowed Priorat to find its place almost immediately within the landscape of great international wines: at the beginning of 1990 the Spanish production landscape featured some important red wines of Roja often characterized by a particular passage in wood; that is why, thanks also to their expressive originality, Priorat wines have managed to leave an impression on consumers' palates, especially those of the French.

Nowadays Priorat is one of the most sought-after territories in the entire country; its denomination has literally transformed within a few decades, attracting strong investments from all over Spain and beyond. What is left intact is the beauty of the landscapes it can offer. In this sun-kissed place, the almost 2,000 hectares of vineyards, often arranged in charming terracing, allow man to pursue a hundred-year old tradition where wine is the protagonist.

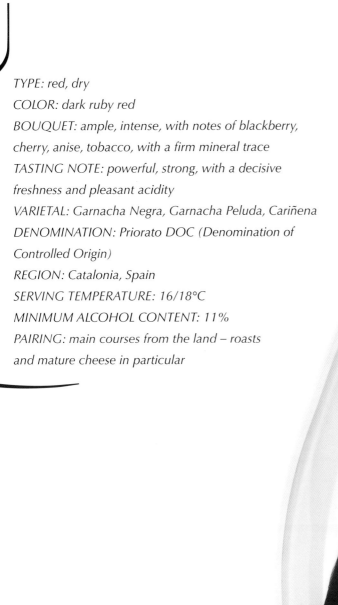

TYPE: red, dry
COLOR: dark ruby red
BOUQUET: ample, intense, with notes of blackberry, cherry, anise, tobacco, with a firm mineral trace
TASTING NOTE: powerful, strong, with a decisive freshness and pleasant acidity
VARIETAL: Garnacha Negra, Garnacha Peluda, Cariñena
DENOMINATION: Priorato DOC (Denomination of Controlled Origin)
REGION: Catalonia, Spain
SERVING TEMPERATURE: 16/18°C
MINIMUM ALCOHOL CONTENT: 11%
PAIRING: main courses from the land – roasts and mature cheese in particular

173

RIBERA DEL DUERO
A GEM IN THE HEART OF CASTILE AND LEÓN

The secret behind the red wines of Ribera del Duero is possibly to be found in several distinct climatic conditions of the region. The area has an altitude of over 700m above sea level and can boast extremely strong temperature ranges, especially in summer. When the sun sets, the scorching heat is easily replaced by temperatures reaching up to 10/15°C: this peculiarity contributes to a strong acidity which is part of the DNA of the best Ribera wines. They are full, bodied red wines with a gustatory development defined by a very dense tannic weft and decisive freshness at the same time. These wines are capable of surprising not only for their elegance but also for their longevity; it is no coincidence that some Ribera wines are put on the market many years after the harvest, much later than any other Spanish or European red wine.

The varietal that is mostly responsible for Ribera del Duero is Tempranillo, locally called Tinto Fino or Tinta del Pais; a varietal that here, as well as in northern Rioja, is able to deliver great, vibrant and deep red wines. However it is the Duero, the long river that stops its run into the Atlantic Ocean and crosses many other important wine-making areas of Spain and Portugal, to characterize the landscape of the area. The Romans were the first to bring vines along the river banks, as a demonstration of the generosity of this area. Nevertheless, if it is possible today to talk about the extraordinary quality of Ribera it is only thanks to the great job carried out by a few botegas up to the early 1980s, when there was a turning point in the history of the denomination. Before then, the quality wine producers could be counted on one hand; barely 24 in 1982, when the denomination was constituted. Today there are over 200, as proof of an almost unrivaled international success. In thirty years, thousands of hectares have been planted; however it is within some of the historical plots of land, some of which are hundreds of years old, that the best grapes are produced; those which make great Ribera del Duero. Unforgettable wines.

TYPE: red, dry

COLOR: ruby red tending to garnet

BOUQUET: ample, complex and deep with balsamic and mineral notes that introduce scents of mixed berries jam, ripened cherry, vanilla and cinnamon, mushrooms

TASTING NOTE: full, powerful, with great balance and harmony

VARIETAL: Tempranillo

DENOMINATION: Ribera del Duero DO (Denomination of Origin)

REGION: Castile and León, Spain

SERVING TEMPERATURE: 16/18°C

MINIMUM ALCOHOL CONTENT: 11.5%

PAIRING: main courses from the land – stewed meats and aged cheese in particular

RIOJA
IN THE NAME OF TEMPRANILLO

The Tempranillo grape is the absolute protagonist of Rioja, the most famous Spanish wine. It is a popular varietal in the entire region and is considered native of the area from Haro, in Rioja Alta, up to Calahorra and Alfaro, in the south, in Rioja Baja. The denomination is situated in the north-east of Spain, south of Bilbao; its grapes come not only from the Autonomous Community of La Rioja but also from a small part of the community of Navarra and the Basque province of Álava.

Tempranillo is capable of producing wines that are as pleasant in their youth as they are charming after a long period of fermentation in barrels and resting in the bottle. They are structured and elegant red wines, always characterized by an irresistibly intense fruity profile. It is no coincidence that the classification of Rioja is based exactly on the period of time that the wine has spent in the cellar before being commercialized. At the base of the quality pyramid of the denomination there are the simple Riojas, also known as "vin joven", young wines: very fresh red wines, always sold one or two years after the harvest and compensating a certain lack of body with an excellent fragrance. A type that is capable of surprising for its immediacy. Immediately above is the classification related to the Crianza wines, whose aging in oak barrels – often having been used before – must last at least 1 year. The best examples of the latter are able to deliver great depth. The Reserva wines, which must remain in the cellar for at least 3 years, of which 1 in oak barrels, are made of the best grapes; it is the type that best represents the denomination, capable of stunning longevity, like all the best wines of the world. Finally, Gran Reserva wines are produced only in the best years and must remain in the cellar for at least 5 years, of which at least 2 spent in oak barrels. There are however a lot of wine makers who in some cases prolong the aging period up to 10 years or so. The result is fantastically structured wines, grand and rich in details at the same time. True masterpieces.

Although the wines from La Rioja are extremely rich in history – there is evidence of the prosperity of the local vineyards dating back as far as the 9th century – the true turning point that shaped their current character occurred with the progressive development of the transport links towards the north, and towards Bilbao and France in particular. The first signs of a certain influence coming from the area of Bordeaux are recorded towards the end of the 1700s, when the first wineries in the area started using huge wooden barrels to age the wines. However it was towards the middle of the 1800s, when the majority of French vineyards went through one of their most dramatic moments because of the Phylloxera, which everything changed: a lot of French négociants started venturing beyond the Pyrenees for wine supplies, much needed for the Bordeaux economy.

Haro, a small town north of the denomination and an important railway stop, hence became a privileged place to harvest and age the wines in Barriques to send them to the north; many of the most important wineries that produce Rioja are in fact still situated right next to the railway track. The productive and cultural intertwining between these areas of Spain and France, lasts in some ways even today and through the decades it has brought many fans of Bordeaux wines to find a cheaper alternative beyond the borders. Throughout a large part of the 1900s, due to the World Wars and the political problems in the country, the wine-making sector in the area struggled to take off again. It is only from the 1960s and 1970s that we have been able to talk of the definitive rebirth of Rioja: still partly influenced by Bordeaux wines, over time they have managed to find an ever increasing personality, becoming a point of reference for the entire Spanish production sector. It is therefore no coincidence that Rioja wines were awarded in 1991 with their first DOCa, the *Denominación de Origen Calificada* (Denomination of Controlled Origin), the highest quality certification for the classification of Spanish wines.

TYPE: red, dry
COLOR: ruby red tending to garnet
BOUQUET: intense with notes of cherry, blackberry and violet.
Scents of vanilla, leather and tobacco
TASTING NOTE: full, elegant, great balance between body
and fragrance
VARIETAL: Tempranillo
DENOMINATION: Rioja DOCa (Denomination of Controlled Origin)
REGION: La Rioja, Navarra, Basque Country
SERVING TEMPERATURE: 16/18°C
MINIMUM ALCOHOL CONTENT: 11.5%
PAIRING: main courses from the land – roasts and aged cheese in
particular

SAINT-ÉMILION
THE OVERWHELMING DEPTH OF THE RIGHT BANK

If we could give a date of birth to Bordeaux wines, it would probably coincide with the arrival of the Romans in the region. In the area of the current Saint-Émilion they started planting those varietals from southern France and produced a wine that would be preserved in terracotta amphorae. This practice would last for centuries, managing to survive even after the fall of the Empire, despite a historical context of huge uncertainty. Like in many other areas of France, it is no coincidence that it was thanks to the local monastic orders that production continuity was possible and it was destined to survive through most part of the Middle Ages. For instance starting from the 11th century, the Benedictines laid the foundations of the wines we know today, thanks to long painstaking work on varietals and cultivation techniques. Moreover, the fragmentation of the vineyards typical of the whole denomination of Saint-Émilion has its roots in the many small and tiny farms in the Middle Ages, when wine was allocated to an almost exclusive household consumption. A significant turning point happened initially in the 14th century with the first expeditions to England and then afterwards starting from the 18th century; an ever growing interest for Bordeaux red wines generated studies on agronomic techniques and on the different characteristics of the production areas. The concept of Crus comes to life, i.e. a vineyard which is specifically dedicated to producing a superior quality wine. Overall this is a region unique for its geological and climatic characteristics, and producing outstanding wines.

In 1855 the attention on Bordeaux wines was mainly focused on the area of Médoc; that is the reason why Saint-Émilion wasn't included in the famous classification requested by Napoleon III. It took 100 years to get to something similar, not long after the denomination was created in 1936: unlike the one of Médoc, its classification is periodically updated, so that it can best represent the productive layout of the area. This way each château in Saint-Émilion is pushed to improve and so it feeds a constant productive "tension" which is particularly positive in the entire region. Reviewed in 1969, 1986, 1996 and 2012, at the top of the classification pyramid are the Premier Grand Cru Classé A, i.e. those wineries whose production consistency has no equal, immediately followed by the Premier Grand Cru Classé and the Grand Cru Classé.

Unlike the so-called left bank of the Gironde, the area of Saint-Émilion is not dominated by the Cabernet Sauvignon varietal, as it would struggle to reach a perfect ripening because of the continental climate, less influenced by the Atlantic Ocean. The Merlot and Cabernet Franc varietals are the backbone of most wines in Saint-Émilion: structured, rounded and velvety red wines with peculiar depth and undoubted charm.

Although the area dedicated to production is quite vast, it is actually around the namesake town and in particular towards Libourne where the best Saint-Émilion wines are made. Such a heterogeneous area, featuring soils which can be very different from one another, boasts a hugely varied expressiveness. Not far from where Pomerol is produced, the north-west enjoys excellently elegant and refined wines, supported by Cabernet Franc as a predominant varietal. In the area east of Saint-Émilion, on a plateau that fades towards St-Laurent, it is possible to come across wines which are generally less fruity and intense, but not necessarily less pure. They are ample, generous red wines, which can surprise with their incisiveness and longevity. These are elements of all the best Saint-Émilion; wines that can be appreciated even after decades have passed.

The best French Cabernet Franc-based wines are found in Saint-Émilion (Bordeaux) or in the area of Touraine, in the Loire Valley.

TYPE: red, dry

COLOR: intense ruby red

BOUQUET: ample, rich, with notes of currant, blackberry, ripened cherry, black cherry jam, vanilla and licorice

TASTING NOTE: rounded, velvety, pleasantly soft and with great persistence

VARIETAL: Merlot, Cabernet Franc

DENOMINATION: Saint-Émilion AOC (Appellation of Controlled Origin)

REGION: Bordeaux, France

SERVING TEMPERATURE: 16/18°C

MINIMUM ALCOHOL CONTENT: 11%

PAIRING: main courses from the land – roasts and aged cheese in particular

TAURASI
CHARACTER, DEPTH, ELEGANCE

The origin of the name "Aglianico", the varietal at the heart of Taurasi, is anything but certain. As an ancient one, it is possible that it is to be linked to "Vitis ellenica", the expression used by the Romans to define its genesis. Other sources connect it to Elea, ancient city in Magna Graecia situated along the Tyrrhenian coast not far from Salerno, and to the subsequent Aragon denomination, hence the current pronunciation. Others believe it could come from a dialectal form used up until the middle of the 1800s: "a glianica" or "grapes of the plain", the one produced in the plainest areas of Campania.

Surely Aglianico is by far the most important varietal of south Italy. Over the centuries it has managed to adapt to many different areas, delivering excellent results everywhere. At least 3 denominations between Camani and Basilicata have it as a protagonist: Taurasi, Aglianico del Taburno and Aglianico del Vulture. Amongst them, the first one is the most important; it is in the vast area known as Irpinia that Aglianico has demonstrated to be able to deliver wines, extraordinary for detail, energy and longevity. The origin of these features is mainly to be found in the continental climate in the province of Avellino, which allows the grapes to have plenty of time to reach a perfect ripening: here the harvest is generally planned for the second half of October.

Aglianico's history is full of anecdotes and stories, the most important of which is the one that sees it gaining a prominent position during a particularly difficult historical period. Whilst half of Europe was dealing with the damage caused by Phylloxera – an insect that destroyed the vineyards in the continent between the middle and the end of the 1800s – many denominations managed to continue their production thanks to the large supplies of red wine coming from Campania. Because of the particular soils in the area, the Phylloxera showed up relatively later than in other wine making areas, therefore guaranteeing the survival of the entire wine production sector. Then the enlightened work of the local institute for agriculture guaranteed the necessary continuity throughout the most part of the 1900s.

Nowadays Taurasi – a small municipality of 3,000 inhabitants that can boast the first DOCG (Denomination of Controlled and Guaranteed Origin) of south Italy since 1993 – represents one of the most prominent production areas in the country. Its wine is universally recognized as one of the great Italian red wines, witnessing a growing attention mainly thanks to the extraordinary results achieved by its best interpreters. Decisive and vigorous, it possesses a dense tannic weft, good freshness and great gustatory persistence. Capable of complementing meals on the most diverse occasions, it can unveil a unique elegance even many years after the harvest.

It is dark ruby red, opening up to a fresh yet dense taste, with notes of cherry and violet, along with light and pleasant scents of licorice and vanilla. Savory, full and energetic on the palate, it recalls mineral hints that deliver a particular expressive vitality.

TYPE: red, dry

COLOR: dark ruby red

BOUQUET: ample and deep with notes of cherry, black cherry, plum (even as a jam), violet, licorice, vanilla and tobacco

TASTING NOTE: energetic, full, lively, moderately tannic and slightly savory

VARIETAL: Aglianico

DENOMINATION: Taurasi DOCG (Denomination of Controlled and Guaranteed Origin)

REGION: Campania, Italy

SERVING TEMPERATURE: 16/18°C

MINIMUM ALCOHOL CONTENT: 12%

PAIRING: main courses from the land – stewed game, roast and aged cheese in particular

ZINFANDEL
AN AMERICAN STORY

The most famous Californian wine is Cabernet Sauvignon, a red that in fifty years or so has managed to show incredible substance and elegance, as well as challenging the best wines from Bordeaux and the rest of the world. Additionally the State has always been known for a particularly rich wine, much more widespread in the past than in recent years, revered by a wide circle of aficionados for its unique peculiarities: Zinfandel. It is a great classic, known by everybody and rightly considered the most characteristic wine of a large part of California.

The history of the namesake varietal is rich in anecdotes about its origin; for years it wasn't clear what varietal it exactly was and where it came from. Certainly the Zinfandel varietal started to spread in the north of California since the first half of the 1900s, when it started being appreciated for its productivity and vigor. Several ampelographers put their heads together in researching the Zinfandel varietal without making great progress: never seen before, it was certainly different from all those popular ones coming from France at that time. The only thing that was discovered was its arrival to the United States; in 1829 it landed on the eastern coast directly from Vienna and the Austrian Imperial nursery, along with many other plants from that area. This halo of mystery lasted for several decades up to the end of the 1960s when the plant pathologist and wine expert Professor Austin Goheen of the UC Davis was the first to suggest an exciting correlation with Primitivo, a red skinned grape vastly diffused in Apulia, the heel of Italy. At the end of the 1980s, with the expansion of the genetic profiling of the grapes, all doubts were swept away: Zinfandel and Primitivo were twin brothers.

How it arrived from Apulia to the Unites States was still unknown. Everything cleared up in 2001 when a few plants of a nearly extinct varietal were found in Croatia: the Crljenak Kaštekanski was a varietal genetically comparable to Zinfandel, as well as to the Primitivo. This incredible story tells not only the genesis of a varietal but also of all the difficulties that have populated the recent history of ampelography, the discipline that studies, identifies and classifies the wine varietals from all over the world.

The Zinfandel we know today is a particularly warm, intense red with a fruity profile of undoubted charm: blackberry, blueberry, prune and currant are only a few of its many recognizable traits. It is a rich and charming wine, often used to blend with some of the most interesting Californian red wines.

TYPE: red, dry
COLOR: intense ruby red
BOUQUET: fruity, with intense scents of cherry, prune, blueberry even as jam, black pepper, licorice, vanilla and smoked tobacco
TASTING NOTE: deep, warm, with a good structure
VARIETAL: Zinfandel
DENOMINATION: Napa Valley
REGION: California, USA
SERVING TEMPERATURE: 16/18°C
MINIMUM ALCOHOL CONTENT: approximately 12.5/13%
PAIRING: main courses from the land – aged cheese, grilled meat and stuffed pastries in particular

THE INFINITE NUANCES
OF SWEET WINES

Although representing a minimal percentage of global production and consumption, the category of sweet wines is unique for the charm that some of its examples possess. With thousands of different hues, these wines can delight with the intensity and variety of their scents: dried and candied fruits, honey and jam, caramel, syrup and even toasted and spicy notes. All these aromas can be discovered again upon tasting, along with a subtle and enthralling sweetness, as well as a great balance of strong freshness and a certain body. Overall these characteristics deliver wines which not only are exceptionally good but are also incredibly long lived and capable of challenging the passing of time.

Many of them are produced from dried grapes, sometimes harvested a few weeks late – during which they naturally lose part of their weight, so concentrating sugar and aromas – or left to rest after the harvest on specific racks. Some of them benefit from a particular rot that in certain climatic conditions covers the berries and unmistakably defines their aromatic profile during the vinification. Sauternes wines, from the Bordeaux region, are the most famous. Others are actually born from grapes which are harvested only in winter, once they are covered in frost. Some of the best Icewines come from North America but there are also excellent versions being produced in Germany, Austria and throughout continental Europe. Last but not least, let's not forget another peculiar category, i.e. fortified wines: being both dry or sweet and white or red, they have a percentage of distilled alcohol or acquavite. Their history is closely linked to the multiple events that happened in Europe throughout the centuries. These wines were created to reach the tables of the European upper classes, the English in particular. That is why the Jerez de la Frontera port in Andalusia, the Marsala port in Sicily and Porto in Portugal are synonymous with great wines. Going through multiple vicissitudes, these wines have managed to reach us today thanks to a solid tradition and, in some cases, thanks to the input of enlightened wine makers.

They are ideal to complete a nice dinner, as well as a perfect accompaniment to the best desserts or enjoyed on their own as meditation wines. They enable us to travel through time and space like no others.

ICEWINE
THE COLD AS A FAITHFUL ALLY

An extraordinary dessert wine, Icewine comes from those areas of the world with a particularly bitterly cold climate. It is a unique wine which simply cannot be reproduced anywhere else, as it is obtained from grapes that are left to freeze naturally on the plant, in the vineyard. This procedure results in a particularly intense juice, rich in extracts and sugar. Although the story goes that it all started in Germany in 1794 (after a premature and sudden frost, the farmers tried to save their harvest by trying to make wine out of the frozen grapes), it was actually Canada and in particular the province of Ontario, the area with that reliably particular climatic stability which assures the quality of the wine, along with a stable production continuity.

Everything starts when it is decided to harvest only part of the grapes, leaving the rest to continue their ripening under progressively decreasing temperatures. This is a crucial and delicate period, as potential hailstorms or specific diseases could irreversibly harm the following harvest. The harvest starts when the temperature is stable below zero, so that the grapes are taken to the cellar whilst still frozen.

What is surprising about this process is the extremely low yield of the grapes: just as an example, in order to obtain 1 liter of Icewine it could be necessary to use up to 10 kg of grapes, almost 7-8 times more than a normal white wine. The result is however a unique product, with a beautiful color ranging from gold to amber, and a charming bouquet: honey, caramel, ginger, peach, apricot and candied citrus are only a few of the notes that characterize its best interpretations.

Canadian Icewine is historically produced from Riesling and Vidal Blanc varietals; the latter, which is gaining more and more appreciation, is a hybrid varietal that brings high levels of sugar and moderate acidity. Some wine-makers use also Chardonnay and Gewürztraminer grapes. More recently there have been small productions of Icewine from Cabernet Franc, one of the most important varietals of the Bordeaux region.

TYPE: white, sweet
COLOR: golden yellow
BOUQUET: intense and deep with notes of honey, caramel, ginger, lychee, pineapple, papaya, candied citrus
TASTING NOTE: sweet, complex, captivating, with a pronounced aroma and slight acidity
VARIETAL: Riesling, Vidal Blanc
DENOMINATION: Icewine
REGION: Ontario, Canada
SERVING TEMPERATURE: 11/13°C
MINIMUM ALCOHOL CONTENT: 7%
PAIRING: ideal at the end of the meal with custard-based desserts and foie gras in particular

MARSALA
A FASCINATING STORY

It has been several years since Sicily seems to have discovered her production vivacity again. The whole region now enjoys a new generation of wine makers who, along with the long-established ones, seem capable of endorsing its most traditional peculiarities in a uniformed way. If this is true for Etna, which is perhaps the most multifaceted of the Sicilian denominations, it is equally true for all the main wine regions, from Vittoria to Noto, from Faro to Menfi, from Alcamo to the Aeolian Islands. Furthermore, an area which seems on the verge of regaining the glory of its past is Marsala, an enchanting location at the western end of the island. It is a special place that gives its name to one of the most world-famous Sicilian wines and is one of the most important Italian products for its history and diffusion.

Everything started in 1773 when the vessel of English trader John Woodhouse, possibly because of the weather, was diverted into the port of Marsala. Once in town, he and his crew had the chance to taste the wine that had been historically produced in the hinterland; a white, rich in history and appreciated for its unique traits since Roman times. It was traditionally left to age in large wooden casks that were never emptied: only a part of their content was taken out every time a younger one replaced it. This way the casks would always contain the right proportion of wines of different vintages. Woodhouse found that the charismatic wine had some similarities with certain white wines from Spain and Portugal, so popular at that time in England. He planned to ship a few dozen Pipes (small 412-liter barrels) over there; however before doing so, he added some distilled alcohol in order to guarantee the preservation of the wine during the long journey through the Strait of Gibraltar. He didn't know then that the modern Marsala was born exactly at that moment.

Its success was immediate and so vast that Woodhouse returned to Sicily to settle and start mass production. After a few years, Marsala received extraordinary fame, which attracted many others to invest in that territory, bringing the wine to tables all over the world. However, during most part of the 1900's Marsala saw a progressive decline. It was only towards the end of the century, thanks to increased attention towards the entire production process, that it started making a comeback.

Marsala boasts a classification that can appear complex but one that perfectly describes its excellence. The wine can be Ambra, Oro or Rubino, depending on the grapes used for its production. The first 2 are made with white varietals, such as Grillo, Catarratto or Inzolia. The last one is produced with red varietals such as Pignatello, Nero d'Avola or Perricone. Furthermore, Marsala wine can be classified as Fine, Superiore, Superiore Riserva, Vergine, Vergine Riserva or Vergine Stravecchio, depending on the duration of the aging process, respectively from the shortest to the longest. Finally, the last criteria of classification is related to its sweetness: Secco, Semisecco or Dolce.

In 1773 the foundations of a recipe which fundamentally has remained intact throughout the centuries, were laid. Marsala has remained a fortified wine, i.e. it is always complemented by a certain quantity of distilled spirit during its production. At the same time, a small group of wine makers are currently recreating the old tradition of the local white, prior to Woodhouse, with extraordinary results of depth and longevity. In both cases this world should be ventured into with as much a curiosity as possible; Marsala is able to surprise with its range, details and depth. Not bad at all.

TYPE: red and white, dry and sweet
COLOR: golden yellow often tending to amber, ruby red
BOUQUET: intense and rich, with notes of broom,
orange blossom, candied and dried fruit, tobacco,
cocoa, almond, licorice
TASTING NOTE: warm, persistent, captivating,
with great persistence
VARIETAL: Grillo, Catarratto, Nero d'Avola, Perricone
DENOMINATION: Marsala DOC (Denomination
of Controlled Origin)
REGION: Sicily, Italy
SERVING TEMPERATURE: 10/12, 14/16°C
MINIMUM ALCOHOL CONTENT: 17.5%
PAIRING: ideal at the end of the meal with biscuits,
dry patisserie and dried fruits

PASSITO DI PANTELLERIA
WIND, SEA AND LIGHT

When strolling in Pantelleria one has the perception of being in a very special place: a tiny spot on the map, closer to Tunisia than to Italy, where the sweet yet impetuous Mediterranean Sea meets a unique, raw land, rich in historical significance. The island is shaped by the wind and illuminated by a sun shining so brightly that it appears painted upon the sky.

Passito di Pantelleria undoubtedly reflects the character of the island. It is a wine of extraordinary charm, sweet yet energetic, with vast depth. Its history is believed to go back a thousand years; in 200 BC Mago, a Carthaginian General, described its production: "Well-ripened bunches of grapes were picked and separated from the mildewed ones. They were laid on a reed and put under the sun to dry, taking care to cover them at night time to keep the dew off. Once dried, the grapes were placed into a jar and covered with must. After six days, they were pressed and all the juice collected. Next, the pomace was treaded and fresh must obtained by other sun-dried grapes, was added. Finally, the wine was sealed in clay vessels, which would be opened after a fermentation of twenty to thirty days…". The modern process of making Passito di Pantelleria is not that different from the past: after the harvest, which usually takes place during the month of August to make the most of the strong summer heat, the grapes are left to rest in the open air on mats of reed for a few weeks, often turned onto the other side in order to make the withering as uniformed as possible. Next the grapes are added to the must obtained from the second part of the harvest; it's at this moment they rehydrate so that they boost not only the sugar but also all those aromas that make Passito di Pantelleria so special within the range of the so-called meditation wines. A further phase of cellar maturation and refining in the bottle create a final wine of aromatic complexity and incredible intensity. A special wine to share with special people.

Not just Pantelleria: volcanic soils are the foundation of some of the most characteristic Italian wines, from the area of Soave (Veneto) to Etna (Sicily).

TYPE: white, sweet

COLOR: intense golden yellow

BOUQUET: rich, with notes of apricot jam, dates, figs, almonds, candied citrus, orange blossom honey

TASTING NOTE: sweet, enthralling, with a pleasurable acidity and great persistence

VARIETAL: Zibibbo (or Moscato di Alessandria)

DENOMINATION: Passito di Pantelleria DOC (Denomination of Controlled Origin)

REGION: Sicily, Italy

SERVING TEMPERATURE: 10/12°C

MINIMUM ALCOHOL CONTENT: 11%

PAIRING: at the end of the meal, with dry patisserie and jam tarts in particular

PORT
DUORO AND A WINE THAT MADE HISTORY

Although in recent years the entire region of Duoro in north-east Portugal has attracted attention for a decent production of dry wines, its fame is undoubtedly related to its most representative product: Port. It is one of the most important wines in the world: its name comes from the namesake naval and commercial town – Porto – from where barrels coming from the hinterland have been shipped to England for centuries. The production area follows the course of the river Duoro, which was a privileged wine transportation route towards the town up to a few decades ago. From a naturalistic point of view, it is a stunning territory, with steep hills that seem to be about to dive into the river that has carved a deep canyon below over hundreds of years. Here, man has demonstrated great expertise by terracing, thus creating unique landscape contours; it is not unusual to come across vineyards the configuration of which dates back to the 17th century.

The history of Port itself, like that of many other fortified wines from Sherry to Marsala, is closely linked to the commercial routes. Although the Vitis vinifera was already widespread in the area at the time of the Romans, the English were actually the ones to pick up production and improve it from the end of the 17th century onwards. Like in other cases, the problem was mainly transportation; to make sure that the wine could face the long journey, it was usual at that time to add a small percentage of brandy to each barrel, so that the alcohol would stabilize the wine profile and guarantee its integrity throughout the duration of the trip. Is that true? Another version gives the paternity of this invention to the monks of the Duoro region, who used to add a small percentage of spirit during the fermentation process. This would make the wine more long-lived and warmer but also sweeter, as not all the sugar would disappear by turning into alcohol. What is certain is that over the centuries the production techniques have been honed and have given life to a type of wine that has no equals anywhere else; its historical peculiarity has sweetness and alcohol coexisting in a perfect balance that contributes to make Port one of the most charming wines in the world.

Port is not produced only in one type; over time many other styles have emerged and contributed to its fortune, from the simplest and more immediate version to the richest one that spends a longer time in the production cellar. Although also available in a white version – Porto Blanco – the most relevant local wines come from red grapes. Many are authorized by the product specification, although the predominant varietals are Tinta Barroca, Tinta Cão, Tinta Roriz – know in Spain and in the rest of the world as Tempranillo – Touriga Francesa and Touriga Nacional.

The first and most significant classification refers to the type of wine aging process used: wines left to age in big oak barrels will be rapidly commercialized, whereas those intended for a long period of refining in the bottle could remain in the designated cellar chambers for years or even decades. The easiest and most widespread is Ruby Port; with an intense color range of fruity hues, pleasantly sweet and with an easy gustatory profile, it is certainly not suitable for long periods of aging in the bottle.

Another popular category is Tawny Port, ideal for those wanting to begin experiencing the main characteristics of the local wines: fruity notes blend with sweet hints of walnuts and almonds that recall the oxidation. However, it has nothing to do with Tawny Aged wines; these are aged longer and can delight with their longevity as well as with their vastness and depth. The Vintage ones, in all

TYPE: red, sweet

COLOR: dark ruby red

BOUQUET: deep, with notes of blackberries and currant jam, dried fig, hazelnut, cocoa, coffee, sandalwood, tobacco, leather and vanilla

TASTING NOTE: sweet, captivating, full, deep, with great persistence

VARIETAL: Touriga Nacional, Tinta Barroca, Tinta Roriz, Tinta Cão, Touriga Franca

DENOMINATION: Port DO (Denomination of Origin)

REGION: Duoro Valley, Portugal

SERVING TEMPERATURE: 14/16°C

MINIMUM ALCOHOL CONTENT: 16.5%

PAIRING: for meditation

their declinations – especially the famous Late Bottled Vintage (LBV) – represent the most important category, at the top of the complicated qualitative pyramid of Port.

They are dense and intensely colored wines, reaching even garnet hues. Their aromas are unique, from scents of fruit jam to withered flowers: hazelnut, walnut husk, cocoa, chocolate and coffee. And again, tobacco, leather and even a rainbow of spices, not only oriental. These Port wines can surprise even after decades; some of the oldest bottles, really well preserved and unopened, come from the region of Duoro. They can overwhelm with their perfectly harmonious balance of warmth and sweetness, which captivate yet never tire the tasting experience, thanks to an unexpected freshness, reaching a finale of incredible duration and gustatory precision in the best cases.

RECIOTO DELLA VALPOLICELLA
TRADITION IN THE NAME OF SWEETNESS

Without a doubt, Valpolicella is one of the most important territories for Italian wine: a relatively vast area that stretches north of Verona and looks out to Lake Garda on one side and to the Soave and Gambellara denominations on the other, towards Vicenza. Here, thanks to a lucky combination of climatic and geological factors, the grapes have found their home. It is in these valleys that they always deliver extraordinarily charming and original wines. It is no coincidence that the name itself, Valpolicella, seems to come from the Latin "vallis-polis-cellae", "valley with many cellars": between the 4th and 5th century, the Roman politician, historian and intellectual Cassiodorus, who was Minister of Theodoric, king of Visigoths, described in one of his letters a wine called Acinatico, produced in this exact area and obtained through a specific withering process. It was the precursor of the wine we know today.

Recioto is the most traditional of all wines produced in Valpolicella. Sweet, warm and pleasantly structured, Recioto is the result of a long and delicate process which starts with the harvest then goes to the drying of the grapes for a period that can last up to 3 or 4 months. For practical reasons, nowadays the grapes are left to rest inside wooden cases one on top of the other or, with ever growing frequency, in plastic cases. The tradition kept alive with pride by a handful of producers, would dictate that the grapes are hung one by one with a small hook to a complicated system of ropes placed horizontally and vertically. This is the only way the grapes can wither in the best possible conditions.

The drying of the grapes takes place in dedicated chambers, called "frutta" (literally, chambers for fruit), normally situated above the cellars up in the hills in order to benefit from the best weather conditions: a low level of humidity and special ventilation. During such a long period, the grapes lose a significant part of their weight, concentrating those sugars that will be afterwards recognizable in the glass, once vinification is complete.

Intense, complex and with great persistence, Recioto della Valpolicella can be also produced in an interesting sparkling version. As protagonist of festive occasions in both versions, it is a particularly evocative wine, forever linked to the traditions of Valpolicella.

TYPE: red, sweet
COLOR: dark ruby red, intense and cryptic
BOUQUET: complex and deep with spicy notes of blackberry, plum, black cherry jam, cocoa, licorice, menthol
TASTING NOTE: sweet, soft, warm and captivating, with great persistence
VARIETAL: Corvina, Corvinone, Rondinella
DENOMINATION: Recioto della Valpolicella DOCG (Denomination of Controlled and Guaranteed Origin)
REGION: Veneto, Italy
SERVING TEMPERATURE: 14/16°C
MINIMUM ALCOHOL CONTENT: 12%
PAIRING: ideal at the end of the meal, as a company to dry patisserie and spicy desserts in particular

SAUTERNES
NOBLE ROT AS A DISTINCTIVE TRAIT

Universally considered the most famous and best sweet wine in the world, Sauternes can claim an unrivaled history and prestige. Although the legend goes that the first wines from "nobly rotten" grapes were produced around the middle of the 1600s in Hungary, in the famous area of Tokaji, the charm of the sweet wines produced in the Bordeaux region has for centuries made its way to all the most important tables of Europe first, and then of the world. As a wine of incredible richness conquering generations of nobles, the enthusiasm towards it has done nothing but fuel its myth. In 1855, when the famous classification of Bordeaux was created, the area of Sauternes was the only one outside Médoc to be included in that list, still held in such a high esteem nowadays. Moreover, for some vineyards producing solely Sauternes they introduced the denomination Premier Cru Supérieur to underline its excellent quality.

In the entire area, 5 municipalities are authorized to produce Sauternes; Barsac, the biggest, Bommes, Fargues and Preignac, as well as the one bearing the same name. They are all near the Ciron, a river that flows further north into the Garonna. Unlike the Bordeaux region, these areas are characterized by a slightly colder climate in winter and hotter in summer, southwards influenced also by the vast Landes forest. All these subtle differences together create a unique microclimate; with the arrival of fall, it supports the formation of those mists that are the primary cause of the pourriture noble (noble rot), peculiarity of all Sauternes wines. At night the humidity helps the formation of a specific rot called *Botrytis Cinerea* on the skins of the Sémillon, Sauvignon Blanc and Muscadelle grapes (the most popular and important varietals of the area); the rot envelopes and protects the grapes from other diseases. Some châteaux, especially those which are more attentive to the quality of their wines, come to harvest their vineyards even up to 5 times: at each passage, they pick up only the grapes completely wrapped up in the rot. What might apparently seem a disease, actually manages to favor the discharge of water from the grapes, bringing therefore the sugar to concentrate and delivering an aromatic profile of rare originality and intensity.

The wine is a particularly precious nectar. Apart from giving Sauternes the unique aromatic profile, the noble rot also contributes to a drastic reduction of yield per hectare; that is why the prices of the wines are so high once they hit the market. The cost is however justified by the unique notes that the best Sauternes can give. The hints of honey, saffron, candied fruit and citrus are able to evolve with nobleness throughout the years if not decades, making Sauternes wines the most long-lived in the world.

TYPE: white, sweet

COLOR: gintense golden yellow

BOUQUET: intense with notes of honey, saffron, orange jam, candied fruit, vanilla, pepper, cinnamon and hazelnut

TASTING NOTE: sweet, soft, captivating, with a vibrant freshness and great persistence

VARIETAL: Sémillon, Sauvignon Blanc, Muscadelle

DENOMINATION: Sauternes AOC (Appellation of Controlled Origin)

REGION: Bordeaux, France

SERVING TEMPERATURE: 11/13°C

MINIMUM ALCOHOL CONTENT: 13%

PAIRING: ideal at the end of the meal with foie gras and blue cheese in particular

SHERRY
THE INTENSITY OF GREAT CLASSICS

Although the vast area surrounding Jerez de la Frontera can claim a particularly productive range of diverse types of wines, without doubt the collective imagination knows it above all for one of the most acclaimed fortified wines in the world: Sherry.

Known in Spain under the name of Jerez and in France as Xérès, Sherry is named after the namesake Andalusian town, where the Iberian Peninsula faces Gibraltar and Morocco. It is a place of incredible allure, a melting pot of cultures where wine has always played a crucial role. For example there are many documents that are testimony to how much the local produce, at that time only sweet, was appreciated in Rome, which was the capital of the empire Andalusia belonged to. Although the consumption of alcoholic drinks was prohibited during the Moorish domain, a small production managed to survive and to be destined for export towards those countries that weren't under Muslim domination. However it was during that so-called period of "geographical explorations" that Jerez wines knew an extraordinary expansion. The prominent ports of Andalusia, Cadice in particular, were departing points for those ships to conquer the New World and the East Indies. During the supplies embarkation, the vessels were normally loaded with significant quantities of wine: some diaries from that period report that, during one of his expeditions, the famous Portuguese explorer Magellano spent 594.790 *maravedís* for the wine, against the 566.684 spent for the weapons of the ship and the crew. Once the tax on wine export was abolished in 1491, Sherry was finally given prominence, becoming known throughout Europe, especially in England, which hadn't had access to Bordeaux wines anymore because of the long war with France. It is therefore no coincidence that in the following decades many English families decided to move to the surrounding areas of Jerez; this circumstance places Sherry along with other fortified wines which are particularly appreciated in northern Europe – Marsala, Madeira, Port.

Obviously those historical wines were very different from the ones we are familiar with today. Many centuries were needed to hone those techniques that characterize their organoleptic components. What has remained unaltered is the extraordinary *terroir* of Jerez de la Frontera; a very hot and drought-prone region that at the same time benefits from the influence of the nearby Atlantic Ocean.

Moreover, the purity of the best Sherry is found also in the so-called *albariza*; a gypsum-rich soil, light-colored like that found in the Champagne region. It is perfect to retain significant quantities of water and more in general for the cultivation of grapes. Within this context the Palomino – the prominent varietal in the production of Sherry, especially its dry version – manages to reach perfect ripening. A great contribution to the local wines also comes from the Pedro Ximénez varietal and the less common Moscatel, which are normally used for making sweet wines.

The procedure that leads to the birth of Sherry is articulated and certainly fascinating; its classification is amongst the most complex in Europe and is the result of centuries-long expertise. Once the grapes have been vinificated and a first white wine is produced, the *bodegas* of the region have to make the first of many choices, i.e. decide what type of wine it has to become: either Fino or Oloroso, which are the 2 great families included in the denomination (chronologically, the first denomination in the whole of Spain). Fino sherry is generally more delicate, dry, pure and with a certain acidity, whereas the Oloroso variety, although very dry, is darker, more structured and robust, often vinificated in sweet versions. Left to age inside partly emptied barrels, Fino Sherry is characterized by a particular film of natural yeast called *flor* that protects the wine against premature oxidation. Oloroso Sherry also ages through direct contact with air, but it is then fortified until it reaches an alcoholic level of 17-17.5°C; this technique prevents the formation of the film and therefore allows it to oxidate naturally. They are extremely original wines that might have suffered a certain decline in the last decades, mainly due to the scarce quality of the average production. However they seem to be living a true renaissance today. A great Fino is pale white, with a delicate yet full of personality aroma; it can give off charming scents of bread and yeasted dough, hay, citrus and dried fruits. A mineral breath that recalls the sea air opens up to a very dry, refined and rhythmic tasting. Oloroso sherry is completely different, starting from a more marked color that gets close to amber. Notes of oriental spices, polished wood, wax, candied citrus, leather and medicinal herbs can introduce an equally dry and substantial wine; full bodied and multifaceted, it is warm and rounded.

The categories of Sherry don't end there: Manzanilla, Amontillado and Palo Cortado are only some of the names that delight many aficionados worldwide. They are wines worth discovering.

TYPE: red and white, dry and sweet

COLOR: golden yellow, often tending to amber with aging

BOUQUET: intense, ample, with notes of dates, walnuts, figs, candied citrus, ripe apple, olives in brine, withered flowers, chamomile and vanilla

TASTING NOTE: powerful, elegant, with a good freshness and great persistence

VARIETAL: Palomino, Pedro Ximénez, Moscatel

DENOMINATION: Jerez DO (Denomination of Origin)

REGION: Andalusia, Spain

SERVING TEMPERATURE: 11/13°C

MINIMUM ALCOHOL CONTENT: 13.5%

PAIRING: for meditation

TOKAJI
MYTH AND LEGEND THROUGHOUT THE CENTURIES

As a fascinating melting pot of cultures, Hungary boasts a unique variety of grapes and wines. Although hardly known beyond its borders, this richness includes particularly opulent and articulated white wines as well as dynamic and fresh reds. However there is one specific wine that has found its way into the imagination of many enthusiasts and has been appreciated for centuries at the best tables around the world: Tokaji. Gaining its name from the town in the area where it is produced, it had been known as Tokay up until just a few years ago.

As an extremely old wine, its official classification dates back to before that of Bordeaux: it first happened in 1700, then reviewed in 1737 by introducing the classification of the vineyards in first, second and third class, then finally in 1772 with a designated law. On the hills north-east of the country, not far from Slovakia and Ukraine, the first ever botrytized wine was born: a sweet wine produced with late harvested grapes that, thanks to the humidity of foggy mornings, develop a specific rot known as *Botrytis Cinerea*. It is a truly noble rot which reduces the water content and therefore concentrates the sugar as well as the aromas. The result – Sauternes in France is probably the most renowned example – is an unmistakable wine for its harmony, charm, intensity and elegance.

Although the area of Tokay produces excellent dry wines based on Furmint – possibly the most important white varietal of the whole Hungary – its fame is mainly due to Tokaji Aszú, a sweet wine whose production process renders it into a class of its own. The harvest takes place between the end of October and the beginning of November when the grapes, covered in the noble rot – the so-called aszú – are separated from the healthy ones. The latter are then vinificated at the winery to create a dry wine which will later function as a base for the following step. The rotted grapes are left to rest in vats; this way the nectar naturally runs all the way down to the bottom of the mass, creating the base for Eszencia – which is considered to be the most prestigious and distinguished sweet wine of the region. After this crucial step, the aszú grapes are immersed for a few days in the must or in the dry wine, with the purpose of bringing out that sweetness so typical of the best Tokaji. The sugar concentration has a specific classification here: it is measured in puttonyos – the number of vats added to each gönci – the casks of base dry wine.

TYPE: white, sweet

COLOR: golden yellow, often tending to amber with aging

BOUQUET: intense, with notes of dried apricot, candied citrus and sweet spices and honey

TASTING NOTE: sweet, powerful, creamy, with good freshness and excellent persistence

VARIETAL: Furmint, Hárslevelű

DENOMINATION: Tokaji

REGION: Tokaj-Hegyalja, Hungary

SERVING TEMPERATURE: 11/13°C

MINIMUM ALCOHOL CONTENT: 9%

PAIRING: ideal at the end of the meal with foie gras, blue cheese and custard-based desserts in particular

If a Tokaji's label indicates "7 puttoyonos" it means that the wine is sweet, if it says "4 puttoyonos" it is semi-sweet, and so forth.

Nevertheless it is not only the uniqueness of the production process that explains the success of this special wine; it boasts a whole series of stories and legends connected to it, like only few other wines have. One of the stories reveals that it was always available to the powerful rulers throughout Europe because of its alleged therapeutic qualities. Another story goes that Pope Pius IV loved it so much that during the Council of Trent, he stated that it was the only wine deemed "suitable to His Holiness's table". Even Louis XIV of France, after having received it as a gift from the King of Hungary, apparently said: "the king of wines, the wine of kings".

GLOSSARY

IN THE VINEYARD

AGRONOMIST, the person who studies the science and technologies of cultivating the vineyard.

AMERICAN ROOTSTOCK, a vineyard that has been grafted onto the roots of American wild vine, which is naturally resistant to Phylloxera.

CRU, French term that identifies a particular vineyard whose characteristics bring to produce wines, consistent in quality and with traits that set them apart from all the others.

GUYOT, term that indicates one of the most popular vine cultivation methods. It takes its name from the namesake French inventor.

HECTARE, metric unit used in agriculture, equal to 10.000 sq.m – a square with 100 m long sides.

NOBLE ROT, a fungus that attacks the grapes and concentrates their sugar content; it is in certain cases a desired procedure that can deliver the so-called noble rot wines.

PHYLLOXERA, an insect that appeared in Europe for the first time in the 19th century. It causes serious damage to the vine plant, destroying its roots.

UNGRAFTED, a vineyard that hasn't been grafted onto an American vine and has therefore original roots.

VINE ROOT, a vine branch that has roots and can therefore be planted.

YIELD, the production of grapes per a determined vineyard surface, generally measured in quintal per hectare.

IN THE CELLAR

AGING, the process during which the wine improves its organoleptic properties by spending a certain period of time inside specific containers.

ALCOHOLIC FERMENTATION, the chemical reaction that turns the sugar into alcohol and carbon dioxide, thanks to the yeasts inside the must.

AUTOCLAVE, pressurized steel container, of different sizes, used for the production of certain sparkling wines due to its resistance to high levels of pressure.

BARRIQUE, French wooden barrel with a capacity of 225 liters (Bordeaux) or 228 liters (Burgundian).

BATONNAGE, French term that refers to the technique of lees being periodically stirred back into the wine during aging.

CARATELLO, small and robust Italian barrel, which is used for storing specific wines and for balsamic vinegar.

CRÉMANT, French term used to indicate some sparkling wines which have been produced outside the Champagne region.

CUVÉE, French term that indicates the blending of different wines in order to obtain a sparkling wine with homogeneous and stable organoleptic properties.

ETHYL ALCOHOL, the most important alcohol inside a wine, it comes from the transformation of the sugar in the must.

FORTIFIED WINE (or Liquoroso), a wine that has a certain quantity of distilled alcohol added to it, with the purpose of increasing the alcoholic content.

LEES, deposits of yeast and particles that form during the alcoholic fermentation of the must.

MALOLACTIC FERMENTATION, the chemical reaction that turns the strong malic acid into the softer and more pleasant lactic acid, thanks to the action of specific bacteria in the wine.

MILLESIMATO, Italian term that identifies a sparkling wine that comes from grapes of a single harvest.

MUST, the liquid produced by pressing the grapes.

OENOLOGIST, the person who deals with the production of one or multiple wines.

POMACE, the remains of the grapes, including skins and stems.

POTENTIAL ALCOHOL, the alcoholic content that is not final, as a hypothetical result of the fermentation of sugar residue inside the must.

REFINING, the process of leaving the wine to rest inside the bottle, in order to improve its organoleptic characteristics.

SULPHUR DIOXIDE, soluble gas which is added to the must and to the wine with antiseptic and antioxidant properties (by law it can be up to a max of 200 mg/l for white wines and 150mg/l for reds).

TONNEAU, a type of barrel with a capacity of over 500 liters, used for aging the wine.

ON THE LABEL

ALTE REBEN, German term that indicates a wine that comes from notably old grapes.

AOC, Appellation d'Origine Contrôlée, French certification granted to French wines to ascertain the origin and organoleptic properties.

BRUT, a sparkling wine with a sugar residue inferior to 12gr/l.

BRUT NATURE, Dosage Zero or Pas Dosé, a sparkling wine with no addition of sugar after re-fermentation. After disgorgement, only wine with the same characteristics of the one in the bottle, is added.

CONTAINS SULPHITES, mandatory statement for those wines with more than 10mg/l sulphur dioxide (a substance that is almost always added but is also the result of the natural fermentation of the wine).

DEMI SEC, a sparkling wine with a sugar residue between 32 and 50 gr/l.

DO, Denominación de Origen, Spanish certification granted to Spanish wines to ascertain the origin and organoleptic properties.

DOC, Denominazione di Origine Controllata, Italian certification granted to Italian wines to ascertain the origin and organoleptic properties.

DOCa, Denominación de Origen Calificada, Spanish category that includes the best Spanish wine denominations.

DOCG, Denominazione di Origine Controllata e Garantita, Italian category that includes the best Italian wine denominations.

DOUX, a sparkling wine with a sugar residue above 50 gr/l.

DRY OR SEC, a generally sweet sparkling wine, with a sugar residue between 17 and 32 gr/l.

EXTRA BRUT, a sparkling wine with a sugar residue below 6 gr/l.

EXTRA DRY, a sparkling wine which is quite rounded yet its sugar residue is between 12 and 17 gr/l.

VIEILLE VIGNE or VIEILLES VIGNES, French term to indicate a wine coming from old grapes.

IN THE GLASS

ABBOCCATO, Italian term to identify a wine with a subtle sweetness.

AMIABLE, a wine with an element of sweetness.

AMPLE, a rich, complex wine, fascinating for its aromas and taste.

AROMATIC, a wine that clearly resembles the olfactory characteristics of the grapes it has been produced from.

ASTRINGENT, a wine in which an excessive amount of tannins give a dry sensation to the palate, sometimes revealing to be unpleasant.

AUSTERE, a solemn, hard and unfriendly wine.

BALANCED, a wine whose harder and softer parts balance each other in a pleasant feeling of balance.

BITTER, term used to describe a pleasant bitter component, often translating into vegetal notes.

BODIED, a wine which is full, structured and pleasant.

BOUQUET, the ensemble of olfactory sensations that a wine acquires during bottle aging.

BRILLIANT, a wine that is bright and beautiful to look at and reflects the light through the glass vividly.

CLEAR, a wine that doesn't present particles in suspension.

CLOSED, a wine that has spent a long time in the bottle and needs a few minutes to release its best aromas.

CLOUDY, a hazy wine with a substantial quantity of particles in suspension.

CORKY, a wine with a pungent and unpleasant scent and taste, caused by the cork being altered by certain types of rot.

DRY, a wine with no trace of sweet elements.

ELEGANT, a wine with particular class and of great quality.

ETHEREAL, aromas recalling wax or acetone, typical of particularly aged wines.

FLAT, a wine that is not very fresh, with poor acidity and low tannins.

FLORAL, a wine with scents recalling flowers.

FRAGRANT, term that indicates the pleasant scents of younger wines.

FRESH, term used to identify the sensation given off by the acids inside the wine.

FRUITY, a wine with scents that recall fruit.

GENEROUS, a very rich wine, pleasantly soft and ample.

HARMONIOUS, a particularly pleasant wine, with all components in perfect balance.

HERBACEOUS, the sensation of fresh grass or hay in some white and red wines, especially if young.

INTENSE, a wine with a vigorous, marked and sharp fragrance.

MINERAL, term used to identify the sensation given off by the mineral salts inside the wine.

OXIDIZED, term that is used to describe a wine at the end of its evolutionary cycle, dull and with little energy.

PERSISTENT, a wine that leaves a several seconds-long finish on the palate

ROBUST, a particularly structured wine.

ROUNDED, a harmonious wine, soft and rich in glycerin.

SAPID, a wine with a strong mineral trait.

SHORT, a wine that doesn't leave any particular trace on the palate and its flavors disappear rapidly from the mouth.

SILKY, term that identifies a wine that leaves a soft and smooth sensation on the palate.

SOFT, term to identify the structure of the wine that is mellow, enveloping and not aggressive.

SOLID, a rich wine that is not particularly fluid inside the glass, often typical of sweet wines.

SPICY, a red or white wine with scents of spices (sweet and not), especially after a certain aging period inside wooden barrels.

SUBTLE, a wine that is not particularly structured and generally rather fresh.

TANNIC, a wine rich in tannins, i.e. elements that give a certain roughness on the palate.

UNRIPE, a young wine which is not ready yet, whose acidity is still not in perfect balance with the other components.

WARM, a wine that gives off a warm sensation, due to a strong alcoholic content.

WINY, a young wine whose scents recall those of the just pressed grapes; it also indicates the must or wine that have just terminated the alcoholic fermentation.

YOUNG, a wine in progress, whose hard parts are prominent but destined to improve with the passing of time.

THE AROMAS OF WINE

DRY VEGETABLE Scents that recall anything dry, especially grass and leaves. They are typical of aged white wines.

SPICY Popular scents of those wines aged in barrels for a variable period of time; scents of vanilla, cinnamon, cloves, black pepper, nutmeg, etc belong to this category.

UNDERGROWTH Notes linked to the world of vegetable scents and in particular to the world of woods: mushrooms, lichens, musk and truffle. Common in aged red wines.

Any wine is able to release a variable range of aromas and scents, linked to the volatile particles in the glass. A true universe of scents that can be very different from one another, but which by association are reunited in categories of fragrances that are similar to each other.

PATISSERIE Scents that are often linked to the sparkling wine vinification and in particular to the permanent presence of yeasts in the wine; scents of small patisserie, custard, biscuits, etc are commonly detectable.

TOASTED Notes that are linked to the aging of the wine inside wooden barrels and to its evolution inside the bottle; often translating into scents of coffee, almonds, chocolate, tobacco, toasted bread, etc.

FRESH VEGETABLE Scents that are expressed through a green, often not ripened note that recalls peppers, tomatoes leaves, fern, asparagus, etc. They can be found in white varietals such as Sauvignon as well as red varietals such as Cabernet Franc.

DRIED FRUIT *Almonds, hazelnuts, walnuts are all scents that can be especially traceable in sweet wines, produced from white grape varietals. A fascinating world often accompanied by notes of candied fruits and fruit jam.*

FRUIT JAM *A world of scents linked to red and white wines that are often quite evolved; spirited apricot, jams made of cherries, plums, peaches or figs.*

CITRUS *Often linked to young and intense white wines, they can range from lemon to grapefruit, bergamot, cedar and clementines.*

238

FRESH FRUIT A whole range of scents related to red and white wines, often very young – apple, pear, melon, gooseberries, etc.

RED FRUIT Notes that immediately refer to the world of red wines, especially in their first years of life; raspberries, black cherries, cherries, strawberries etc.

TROPICAL FRUIT Often typical of the youngest and most intense white wines, they range from pineapple to banana, from mango to papaya.

239

AUTHORS

FABIO PETRONI was born in Corinaldo, Ancona, in 1964. Currently he lives and works in Milan. After studying photography, he has worked with some of the most celebrated professionals in the field. His career has led him to specialize in portraits and still life, areas in which he has demonstrated an intuitive, precise style. Over the years he has photographed people well-known in the fields of culture, medicine and the Italian economy. He works with the main advertising agencies and has been responsible for many campaigns for important international clients and businesses. For White Star Publishers he has published *Horses: Master Portraits* (2010), *Mutt's Life!* (2011), *Cocktails, Roses* and *Super Cats* (2012), *Orchids, Tea Sommelier* and *Chili Pepper: Moments of Spicy Passion* (2013), *Bonsai* (2014), *Beer Sommelier, a Journey Through the Culture of Beer* (2015) and *Wine Cocktails, New, Creative and Classic Drinks* (2016). He is the official photographer of the IJRC (International Jumping Riders Club) and Young Riders Academy. www.fabiopetronistudio.com

JACOPO COSSATER, born in Veneto, in the north-east Italy, he attended the University in Perugia. It was during this period that he fell in love with Sangiovese, completed his training at the Italian Association of Sommeliers and started his blog, although not necessarily in this order. After extensive training in Milan he came back to Umbria where he currently works. As a journalist he has collaborated on the guidebook *I Vini d'Italia* published by L'Espresso and has been writing on the popular Italian blogs *Enoiche Illusioni* and *Intravino* for many years.

The Publisher would like to thank Luca Castelletti, RIEDEL The Wine Glass Company, Michela Marenco from Marenco Vini, Azienda agricola Santa Giustina and Drei Donà Tenuta la Palazza.

Fabio Petroni would like to thank Simone Bergamaschi, Gloria and Gaia Bucciarelli, Norbert Piovesan, Karl Riegler.

Jacopo Cossater wishes to thank his wife and his family for their constant and inestimable support.

All photographs are by Fabio Petroni except the following: page 46 Siqui Sanchez/Getty

WHITE STAR PUBLISHERS

WS White Star Publishers® is a registered trademark owned by De Agostini Libri S.p.A.

© 2016 De Agostini Libri S.p.A.
Via G. da Verrazano, 15 – 28100 Novara, Italy
www.whitestar.it – www.deagostini.it

Translation: Inga Sempel – Editing: TperTradurre s.r.l.

ISBN 978-88-544-1069-5
1 2 3 4 5 6   20 19 18 17 16

Printed in China